We

Have

Recovered

We Have Recovered

The Common Solution Recovery Program

First printing: May 2010

Stephen J. Baughan, 564 Rinehart Road, Branson, MO 65616

ISBN: 978-0-8922169-9-4
Library of Congress Control Number: 2010927048

Printed in the United States of America

Acknowledgments and special thanks

. . . God

Contents

Contents

God gives us moments and for these
moments we give our lives.
— Fr. Ed Dowling

PREFIX

*To show other alcoholics precisely
how we have recovered is the main
purpose of this book.*[1]

Schindler's List is a 1993 film about a German business-man, Oskar Schindler, who saves the lives of over a thousand Polish Jewish refugees by employing them in his factories to avoid the German concentration camps and escape certain death. The movie was a box office and critical success, winning numerous awards, including Best Picture and a Best Director Oscar for Stephen Spielberg. Schindler, despite all he has done, is weeping at the end of the production wishing that he could have saved "one more."

Many people have asked me why *We Have Recovered* was written. "After all," they say, "what you folks are doing now is helping hundreds of men and women to experience the power of God in finding a way out of the life of addiction to alcohol and drugs. It's working; why mess with it?"

The reasons for placing our program in print are many; at least enough to overcome the disapproval of those who will complain that there is too much mention of God in this book. Or the criticism that will come from those who say that there is too little of Him or that He is called by the wrong name. The objections will include comments that not enough or too much is written about Alcoholics Anonymous. "Where is your treatment plan, where are self-help tips, where is my program?" will come up.

Obviously, *We Have Recovered* was not written to suit the tastes of everyone within the recovery community. That is not possible. It is not written to support my personal recovery program, my sponsor's or yours. *The Common Solution Recovery Program* is written to assist the newcomer in his or her quest to experience the one solution that is offered in the *Big Book of Alcoholics Anonymous.*

Another reason that it has been written is that, as director of the Church Army Branson Program of Recovery for the past several years, I have seen the average age of the newcomer decrease dramatically. I have seen the numbers of females increase at the same time. Those suffering from dual and multiple addictions are at an all-time high. The explosion of those addicted to methamphetamine and prescription drugs, both legal and illegal, has become nearly overwhelming. And lack of adequate help is not being offered in most cases.

The Common Solution Recovery Program that we offer has experienced dramatic success. The seventy-five percent rate of recovery in our program mirrors that which was being experienced in the years following the publication of Alcoholics Anonymous.

The *Big Book*, as it was written in 1939, contained all the information required to recover from alcoholism.

It serves us as the foundation of our program. *We Have Recovered* is merely written to elaborate on and help to clarify a program that has been working for over seventy years. And it is written to include methamphetamine users, opiate addicts, and habitual marijuana users; in fact we have seen the program work on every sort of addiction, including the heroin and crack addicts and other habitual drug users who are suffering right alongside the dying alcoholics.

But the most overpowering personal reason that this book exists is very simply that someday I will stand before God, as will all of us, and give an account for my very existence. For what I did with what I was given. "You used our program to save hundreds and hundreds," might be what I would say. But what will it be like when I hear in reply, "What about the thousands and tens of thousands that were never reached?"

So that is who this text is written for. For those not yet here. And for the thousands who still suffer trapped in a life of addiction. And the many thousands who will follow them. They are what matters, they are who matters. They are all that matter.

Each time someone recovers because they were helped in some way through the publication of this book, there will be one less, "One more."

The human mind has no more power
of inventing a new value than
of imagining a new primary color.
— C.S. Lewis

INTRODUCTION

*The tremendous fact for every one of us is that
we have discovered a common solution.*[1]

"You don't have to keep comin' back to these places." The man who made this comment was visiting a treatment center in Branson, Missouri. He had watched me out of the corner of his eye trying to overhear what he was saying without being noticed. He turned to me and said, "You can recover." I will never forget that moment or those words that God used to change my life forever.

Les had been coming every Saturday afternoon to that place to teach a class on something called the *Big Book* to any of the clients who cared to attend. Few took him up on his offer. I had only attended because a new friend that I had made in that place wanted some company. But what I heard that day has made all the difference in my life. He told us that he came to that recovery center each week because it was a part of his plan for staying sober as instructed in the *Big Book of Alcoholics Anonymous*. He had been coming to offer the clients the three pieces of information that were necessary to recover from alcoholism and other drug addictions. He simply shared the problem, the solution, and the action required to find the solution which he had found, with anyone who cared to have it.

13

His declaration of hope was the origin of this book and the beginning of my personal revitalization. I had come to that place seeking sobriety and, after three weeks, I had found nothing that even remotely sounded like recovery. After all, I reasoned, it *was* called a recovery center. The classes and substance abuse counselors were not offering anything like what he was talking about, nor did the outside meetings that we attended seem to hold out any real hope of change. Until that January day in 1993, I had heard no one even suggest to me that there was such a thing as recovery; that there was a way out, an escape from the disaster that my life had become.

I had come into treatment knowing that I was never going to be able to "not drink" nor was I ever going to be capable of finding control over my drinking and drug use by any method that I had tried thus far. I was the son of an alcoholic. I had watched my father die of cirrhosis of the liver some years earlier; but despite that witness, I had come to the place where I could not stop using alcohol and drugs. It was a position that I had sworn to myself I would never be in on that day that I buried him. I had watched his struggle to stay sober for three years in and out of the rooms of Alcoholics Anonymous, and though he was able to string together a few days, weeks, or even months, he never found a moment's peace while not drinking. I knew what the philosophies and suggestions that he had heard in 1979 were and I knew that I was hearing them again 13 years later. And I knew deep inside that these ideas, well intentioned as they were, would not stop me from returning to drink and drugs at the first opportunity.

That glimmer of hope that was presented to me that day has made all the difference to me, to my family, and many hundreds of others. I asked Les what I had to do and he answered me without hesitation. He said that I was to "Work the steps," not the way that I thought was best, certainly not out of my head or following anyone else's methods, but only in the manner that they were laid out for me in the *Big Book of AA*. Taking those steps was my only chance to survive the fatal illness that I had. Nothing less would do.

And as they say, "the rest is history." Recovery followed the action of doing what the *Big Book* said to do under the guidance and direction of Les and he told me, "If you like what you got, pass it on." And a few months later, I was learning to do just that as I shared what it was like before I recovered, how I recovered, and what life is like now as a recovered alcoholic and drug addict. I learned to share the message of recovery as contained in the *Big Book of Alcoholics Anonymous* with individuals and in group settings and spend much of my time encouraging others to do the same.

As a result of following those directions, I was asked to become the interim director of a small, struggling Christian ministry called Church Army in Branson, Missouri. The Church Army Program consisted of fifteen or so men who were attempting to stay sober and off of drugs by living together in group recovery homes. The turnover in the houses was very high and the results disappointing. Church Army was an organization that had been brought to the Branson area by local business leaders to help the hundreds of working poor who had come to town in search of employment during an economic boom of the early 1990s.

I had no religious background or formalized training and was assisting only because Church Army had discovered while trying to help the working poor of the area that many suffered with substance abuse problems.

In 2004, the focus of the ministry shifted from religious conversion to recovery from alcohol and drug addiction when Church Army began the Common Solution Recovery Classes. The steps of the program of Alcoholics Anonymous, as they were laid out in the *Big Book*, began to be presented in a classroom style setting during weekly two-hour classes. And the miracles began to happen.

The rate of recovery that the *Big Book* promised began to become a realization.[2]

Today, over a thousand men and women have found sobriety and peace in our Common Solution Recovery Program and numerous families have been restored. The hundreds who have come to the classes and worked the steps as presented in the *Big Book of Alcoholics Anonymous* now count themselves among the recovered and restored alcoholics and addicts of the world. They have come to experience the freedom of a life liberated from the tyranny of alcohol and drugs. Transformed lives have become the norm rather than the exception. The stories of some of those changed lives are presented throughout this book. The reason for these astounding recoveries from the despair and hopelessness of alcoholism and drug addiction is twofold.

First, the program of Alcoholics Anonymous, from which the fellowship had acquired its own name,[3] is what these alcoholics and drug addicts are presented with as the solution to their problem. The program offered is the one that became the *Big Book of Alcoholics Anonymous* and was so effective in its early days. The word-of-mouth and sometimes confusing program that is often found today among the fellowship is not what is taught.

When I came to Alcoholics Anonymous I heard many solutions being offered by well-meaning people, none of which were very appealing in light of my problem. I felt confused and discouraged until that man with a book in his hand walked into that classroom and began to teach the AA program of recovery out of the *Big Book* and from his own experience.

The *Big Book of Alcoholics Anonymous* and its message are simple and direct. That message is to follow the directions as laid out and recovery is not only possible but is, in fact, probable. The meetings of AA have always existed to support the program of the *Big Book*. By giving guidance and direction in the working of the Twelve Steps, recovery, defined as a restoration to sanity, is what is offered and, in fact, promised to the newcomer. Bill Wilson, a co-founder of Alcoholics Anonymous himself wrote in a *Grapevine* article in 1958, "The sole purpose of an AA group is sobriety, defined as freedom from alcohol, through the teaching and practice of the Twelve Steps of Alcoholic Anonymous."[4]

Unfortunately, the term "recovery" has become very unpopular in many of the rooms of AA and other Twelve Step groups and has instead been replaced with "recovering" and other expressions that offer little or no hope for the sufferers. Recovery, recovered, and recover are used in the *Big Book* (to describe the alcoholic who has experienced the solution) over 60 times in its first 164 pages while only using the term "recovering" once. And then it is used in describing the view that a spouse has taken of her alcoholic husband.[5]

In many meetings the recovered alcoholic is often chastised and rebuked for calling himself or herself a recovered alcoholic or addict by those in attendance who themselves have claimed the "Don't drink and go to meetings" philosophy of remaining a recovering alcoholic. A substance abuse professional recently shared with a newcomer that the only way that he would ever be a "recovered" alcoholic is when he was "six feet under." That was the message I heard when I came to AA for help and that is the message that is often heard today. However, that is not the message of the *Big Book of Alcoholics Anonymous* or the message of the Common Solution Recovery Program.

Common Solution Recovery has given hope to the newcomer who may have become discouraged in his or her quest to stay sober by their own power while attending meetings where the first step read out loud proclaims, "We admitted we are powerless. . . ." Common Solution Recovery offers some expectation that a brighter future is possible. Through the working of the Twelve Steps and the support of the Common Solution Recovery classes, the seemingly personal failures to stay sober have been explained, optimism has been restored, and recovery has been found.

The second reason that Common Solution Recovery is experiencing a seventy-five percent recovery rate is that the solution offered in the *Big Book* is never compromised. Humanism[6] and the latest fads, styles, attitudes and practices can never be used to replace the fundamentals that worked so well when the *Big Book* was written.

The God-given principles that have governed the world and everything in it are unchanging. The spiritual principles presented in the *Big Book of Alcoholics Anonymous* and the Common Solution Recovery Program are offered as the solution to alcoholism and drug addiction without any religious or theological encumbrances to confuse those seeking an escape from the problem of addiction.

This religious pluralism that allows the atheist and the agnostic, the Christian believer and the non-Christian believer and especially the former churchgoer and the church-damaged to feel welcome and wanted is intentional. But make no mistake. The solution offered in the *Big Book* and the Common Solution Recovery Program is God and God alone. As Bill Wilson said in the *Big Book*, "God is everything or else He is nothing."[7]

The *Big Book* uses the word "God" and many other terms such as Creator, Power, and other descriptive names such as Spirit of the Universe and Creative Intelligence nearly 200 times to describe the Power greater than ourselves necessary to recover. Never does it compromise its message to include any foolish or convenient materialistic replacements that offer comfort to the closed-minded but no recovery. The program as contained in the *Big Book* offers a supernatural solution to an otherwise unsolvable problem.

To do less in the presentation of the Common Solution Recovery material would compromise the message that we know works and has shown the way to real recovery for so many people for so many years. Bill Wilson wrote in the Twelve and Twelve that the Twelve Steps are a set of principles, spiritual in nature, which, if practiced as a way of life, can expel the obsession to drink and enable the sufferer to become happily and usefully whole.[8]

"You can recover" is the promise that I was given by Les that day in 1993. "You can recover" is the promise that Ebby Thacher[9] offered to Bill Wilson in 1934.[10] And "You can recover" is the promise that is made today to everyone who is willing to work the program that is contained in the *Big Book of Alcoholics Anonymous.*

There is hope for the hopeless to find a solution that never fails because God never fails. If alcohol and drugs have beaten you into a state of reasonableness and God has prepared your mind to hear the message contained in the *Big Book of Alcoholics Anonymous,* know that recovery is in your future. My prayer is that this book helps you find the way to that solution.

Know that you can experience recovery and help others to do the same. May God bless you as you embark on your journey to a better way of life.

Poor Pitiful Me

Step One of the Alcoholics Anonymous program was a given for me. I had known for many years that I was powerless over drugs and alcohol and even the men in my life. Obviously, my life was unmanageable as I had no job and was homeless and my kids were either in the custody of the state, in Juvenile Detention or doing dope. I was soon to be on my way to the state penitentiary myself on drug manufacturing charges.

When I got to prison, I began praying the Serenity Prayer, mainly because it was the only one that I knew. I realized that God was getting me through some pretty tough times and I came to believe in Him while locked up. During this time, I came to the realization that I could not return to that old life-style without facing more jail time or a miserable death.

One day in that prison I attended a church service. The preacher was talking about asking to be forgiven for each "individual" sin. That floored me. Through my tears, I began writing down all the wrongs that I had done. Each night I would ask the Lord to forgive me for one of those sins on that list. Little did I know that I was starting on the Fourth Step of Alcoholics Anonymous. It wasn't until I got out and found Church Army Branson and the Common Solution Recovery Program that I began to learn about the steps of Alcoholics Anonymous. I discovered then how crucial it was to work an honest Fourth Step and to share it with someone else in Step Five.

Only then did I see how truly selfish and self-centered I was and how I had been living in fear for so long. I also found out that fear would lead me back to that old lifestyle rather than keep me from it. I realized that I had always blamed someone else for all the things that I was doing wrong. "Poor, pitiful me" was how I had been living for so long. I was so dishonest, yet had always prided myself in telling the truth. Suddenly the real truth was coming to light.

Could God forgive me; could I forgive myself? I was willing enough to give it a shot. So I took that hour that they told me to and began to pray. I didn't really feel any different right away, but others began to tell me that I seemed to be changing. I suddenly began to see the truth in things that were happening, and words were coming out of my mouth that I couldn't believe I was saying. For the first time in my life I was finally beginning to see who I really was.

I remember the first amends that I made was to an old employer that God had placed in my path. I was scared and shaking like a leaf but I knew that I had to go through with it. As I spoke with him about our issues, he let me know that it was okay and that I did not owe him anything. He was even thrilled that I was doing so well. I was so relieved afterward and I began to believe even more what others had told me about working the Common Solution Program of Recovery.

As I grew in my recovery, I began to pray even more. I found that reading and trying to do what the *Big Book* said to do on pages 84–89 gave me a clearer understanding of how to process things as they came up in my life. The amazing thing is when I go back over my day at bedtime, I can't even remember the next day what it was that seemed like such a catastrophe the day before.

Even more amazing to me is when I ask God that if there is someone that needs help to please give me the willingness and direction to help them, He really lays it on me. And, much to my surprise, I am willing and able to do it.

It is with that hope that I realize with gratitude that I am one step closer to Heaven, thanks to God.

It isn't that they can't see the solution.
It's that they can't see the problem.
— G.K. Chesterton

STEP ONE

WHAT IS THE PROBLEM?

*I had met my match. I had been overwhelmed.
Alcohol was my master.*[1]

WHAT IT MEANS TO BE ALCOHOLIC

The term "alcoholic" and "addict" portray many different images to each of us. From the unemployable father to our friend always causing damage to property and people when he was drinking to the homeless bum clutching a brown bag while leaning against a building to stay out of the cold wind. Our mental picture might be the soccer mom who conceals her methamphetamine use from her friends and family or possibly the heroin addict passed out on a filthy mattress or the marijuana-addicted high-school drop-out. Whatever mental portrait we have painted, our depictions will most certainly vary.

There is no attempt made to define or determine what an addict or alcoholic looks like in the pages of the *Big Book of Alcoholics Anonymous*. Bill Wilson never endeavors to classify exactly what an alcoholic is: being married more than twice or having more than one DUI, having been to jail or in prison, or checking into a treatment center or detoxification program so many times are not the measuring stick.

As soon as any attempt is made to define what an alcoholic "is," we know that he or she could and surely would "misidentify."

What the book does attempt to do is to share the personal experiences of many alcoholics in its first chapters to provide the information required to make the necessary mental conclusion that we are alcoholics and cannot manage our own lives; that we are powerless over alcohol and our lives have become unmanageable.

WHY THE ALCOHOLIC IS POWERLESS OVER ALCOHOL

Bill Wilson had discovered the nature of the problem of alcoholism from a depression-era doctor who had treated thousands of alcoholics. As a result, he had developed a theory about what it meant to be "alcoholic" and was asked to share his views on alcoholism. These observations are found in "The Doctor's Opinion" of the *Big Book of Alcoholics Anonymous*.

PURPOSE OF "The Doctor's Opinion"

*In this statement he confirms what we who have suffered alcoholic torture **must** believe — that the body of an alcoholic is quite as abnormal as his mind.*[2]

WHO WROTE "The Doctor's Opinion"?

Dr. William Duncan Silkworth, M.D. was the medical director at Charles B. Towns Hospital, an early 20th century institution for the treatment of alcoholism and drug addiction located in the Manhattan Borough of New York City. This was the hospital where Bill Wilson had been sent seeking treatment for his alcoholism.

My brother-in-law is a physician and through his kindness and that of my mother I was placed in a nationally known hospital for the mental and physical rehabilitation of alcoholics.[3]

Dr. Silkworth wrote two letters for the *Big Book* when asked to contribute his medical expertise in treating drug and alcohol addiction and present his viewpoint of the problem that he had developed while working at the hospital for many years.

A well-known doctor, chief physician at a nationally prominent hospital specializing in alcoholic and drug addiction, gave Alcoholics Anonymous this letter.[4]

Dr. Silkworth had treated many thousands of alcoholics by the time he wrote "The Doctor's Opinion."

He stated that his theory of alcoholism and drug addiction was developed as the result of the men and women he was attempting to help repeatedly asking him the same two questions:

The first question was, "Why can't I stop drinking once I start?"

The first was always followed by another. "Now that I really want to stop altogether, why do I keep starting again? Why can't I stop starting?"

First Question: "Why can't I stop once I start?"

We believe and so suggested a few years ago, that the action of alcohol on these chronic alcoholics is a manifestation of an allergy; that the phenomenon of craving is limited to this class and never occurs in the average temperate drinker. These allergic types can never safely use alcohol in any form at all; and once having formed the habit and found they cannot break it, once having lost their self-confidence, their reliance upon things human, their problems pile up on them and become astonishingly difficult to solve.[5]

---

chronic — continually repeated
manifestation — how something that cannot be seen materializes
allergy — abnormal reaction to a substance
phenomenon — a visible appearance of something without an obvious explanation
craving — morbid demand of the appetite
temperate — moderate, self-controlled

NOTE: The craving is *not* the feeling or thought that occurs when we desire to use. The word is used here to describe what happens after we put alcohol or drugs into our system. Do not translate "craving" into more modern terms such as "jonesing."[6] Throughout "The Doctor's Opinion," the word *craving* always refers to "what happens *after* we use," never before.

PHYSICAL PART OF THE PROBLEM

Dr. Silkworth called this reaction to the substance of alcohol an "allergy." An allergy is an unusual sensitivity to a substance that provokes a reaction different from a person's body that does not have the allergy.

An individual's allergic reaction to penicillin, for example, may result in a swelling of the throat, a rash, vomiting or even death. The only effective treatment for the person who suffers from an allergy to penicillin is to abstain from the use of penicillin. An alcoholic body's reaction to the alcohol is to demand more and more and cannot be satisfied. There is never enough. Like other allergies, the only solution is to not ingest the substance into their body.

First drink = allergy begins; the body demands another drink

Second drink = Allergy is now twice as strong, appetite demanding more, can only be filled with

Third drink = drinking continues unless stopped by an outside force.

First drink or drug = Allergy begins...

Next drink or use = Allergy grows...

Drink or drug use continues = Allergy has control!

This phenomenon, as we have suggested, may be the manifestation of an allergy which differentiates these people and sets them apart as a distinct entity.[7]

> **differentiate** — distinguishes between
> **entity** — unit
> **moderate** — sensible
> **consumption** — intake
> **progressive illness** — more severe over time

He may start as a moderate drinker; he may or may not become a continuous hard drinker; but at some stage of his drinking career he begins to lose all control of his liquor consumption, once he starts to drink.[8]

. . . once the alcoholic takes any alcohol whatever into his system, something happens, which makes it virtually impossible for him to stop. The experience of any alcoholic will abundantly confirm this.[9]

We are convinced to a man that alcoholics of our type are in the grip of a progressive illness. Over any considerable period we get worse, never better.[10]

We are like men who have lost their legs, they never grow new ones. Neither does there appear to be any kind of treatment which will make alcoholics of our kind like other men.[11]

Physicians who are familiar with alcoholism agree there is no such thing as making a normal drinker out of an alcoholic. Science may one day accomplish this, but it hasn't done so yet.[12]

We have seen the truth demonstrated again and again; "Once an alcoholic, always an alcoholic." If we are planning to stop drinking, there must be no reservation of any kind, nor any lurking notion that someday we will be immune to alcohol.[13]

IF THE PHYSICAL ALLERGY IS THE ONLY PART OF YOUR PROBLEM . . . THE SOLUTION IS SIMPLE . . .
DON'T DRINK!

For those who are unable to drink moderately, the question is how to stop altogether. We are assuming, of course, that the reader desires to stop. There was a tremendous urge to cease forever. Yet we found it impossible. This is the baffling feature of alcoholism as we know it — this utter inability to leave it alone, no matter how great the necessity or wish.[14]

If you are among the many who "don't drink" or "don't drink and go to meetings" is not working for, consider the second question that the doctor's patients commonly asked: "Why can't I stop starting?"

THE MENTAL PART OF THE PROBLEM

Men and women drink essentially because they like the effect produced by alcohol. The sensation is so elusive that, while they admit it is injurious, they cannot after a time differentiate the true from the false. To them, their alcoholic life seems the only normal one. They are restless, irritable, and discontented unless they can again experience the sense of ease and comfort which comes at once by taking a few drinks — drinks which they see others taking with impunity. After they have succumbed to the desire again, as so many do, and the phenomenon of craving develops, they pass through the well-known stages of a spree, emerging remorseful, with a firm resolution not to drink again. This is repeated over and over, and unless this person can experience an entire psychic change, there is very little hope of his recovery.[15]

These observations would be academic and pointless if our friend never took the first drink, thereby setting the terrible cycle

injurious — causes harm
differentiate – make a distinction between
impunity — free from consequences
succumbed — given in to
phenomenon — a visible appearance of something without explanation
craving — allergic reaction, morbid demand of the appetite
spree — binge, run
remorseful — sorry
resolution — decision
observations — general descriptions of what happens physically after we drink
academic — waste of time studying

in motion. **Therefore, the main problem of the alcoholic centers in his mind, rather than in his body.**[16]

There is **the obsession** *that somehow, someday, they will beat the game.*[17]

The idea that somehow, someday he will control and enjoy his drinking is the great obsession of every abnormal drinker. The persistence of this **illusion** *is astonishing. Many pursue it to the gates of insanity or death.*[18]

> **illusion** — fixed, false belief

We learned that we had to fully concede to our innermost selves that we were alcoholics. This is the first step in recovery. The delusion that we are like other people, or presently may be, has to be smashed.[19]

If we are planning to stop drinking, there must be no reservation of any kind, nor any lurking notion that someday we will be immune to alcohol.[20]

Young people may be encouraged by this man's experience to think that they can stop, as he did, on their own will power. We doubt if many of them can do it, because none will really want to stop, and hardly one of them, because of the peculiar mental twist already acquired, will find he can win out.[21]

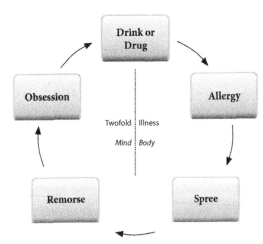

Obsession — A thought or idea more powerful than any other thought or idea that we can retain in our mind; it will absolutely not respond to reason and will always be a lie in the area of the first drink or drug use.

Drink or Drug

Obsession

Allergy

Twofold | Illness
Mind | Body

Remorse

Spree

CYCLE OF ADDICTION

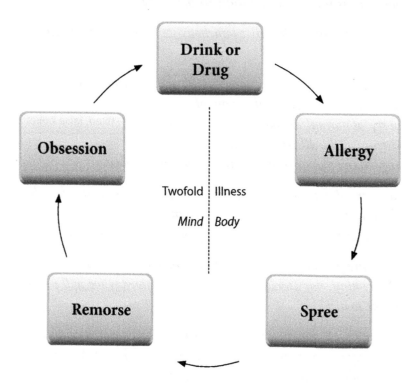

Men and women drink essentially because they like the effect pro-duced by alcohol. The sensation is so elusive that, while they ad-mit it is injurious, they cannot after a time differentiate the true from the false. To them, their alcoholic life seems the only normal one. They are restless, irritable, and discontented unless they can again experience the sense of ease and comfort which comes at once by taking a few drinks — drinks which they see others taking with impunity. After they have succumbed to the desire again, as so many do, and the phenomenon of craving develops, they pass through the well-known stages of a spree, emerging remorseful, with a firm resolution not to drink again. This is repeated over and over, and unless this person can experience an entire psychic change, there is very little hope of his recovery.[22]

So we shall describe some of the mental states that precede a relapse into drinking, for obviously this is the crux of the problem.[23]

> **delusion** — fantasy
> **reservation** — reluctance
> **immune** — not subject to the illness
> **proportion** — cost is too high compared to the benefit
> **mental twist** — obsession of the mind
> **crux** — core

He had much knowledge about himself as an alcoholic. Yet all reasons for not drinking were easily pushed aside in favor of the foolish idea that he could take whiskey if only he mixed it with milk!

Whatever the precise definition of the word may be, we call this plain insanity. How can such a lack of proportion, of the ability to think straight, be called anything else?[24]

*But there was always the **curious mental phenomenon** that parallel with our sound reasoning there inevitably ran some insanely trivial excuse for taking the first drink. Our sound reasoning failed to hold us in check. The insane idea won out.*[25]

*I now remembered what my alcoholic friends had told me, how they prophesied that if I had an **alcoholic mind**, the time and place would come — I would drink again.*[26]

WHY THE ALCOHOLIC'S LIFE IS UNMANAGEABLE

"Bill's Story" in the *Big Book* is written to describe what his life was like while he was drinking, what happened to change his life, and what it was like after the obsession was removed. In it, he offers us examples from his own drinking career of the progressive nature of alcoholism and how the obsession of the mind combined with an allergy of the body nearly destroyed him and the lives of those who loved him.

Drinking was fun for Bill in the early days.

Drink was taking an important and exhilarating part in my life.[27]

Soon, drinking began to cause more serious problems in his life. He was soon drinking only for the effect, the sense of ease and comfort that alcohol brought him. Bill was now drinking for oblivion.

The papers reported men jumping to death from the towers of High Finance. That disgusted me. I would not jump. I went back to the bar.[28]

A short time later, Bill states that he was drinking because he had to.

Liquor ceased to be a luxury; it became a necessity.[29]

Finally Bill tells us that he was drinking gin combined with drugs and had reached the point of "drinking to die."

Next day found me drinking both gin and sedative. This combination soon landed me on the rocks. People feared for my sanity. So did I. I could eat little or nothing when drinking, and I was forty pounds underweight.[30]

Bill had gone from enjoying drinking to drinking for oblivion to drinking because he had to and, finally, to die. He was unwelcome at his former workplaces, unemployable, full of remorse and self-pity, and had become suicidal. His life was obviously unmanageable and yet he continued to drink against all reason and common sense.

Bill admitted to himself that he was an alcoholic. He made the mental conclusion that he was powerless to stop and was doomed to an alcoholic death. He had taken Step One. He writes about this experience in his story.

No words can tell of the loneliness and despair I found in that bitter morass of self-pity. Quicksand stretched around me in all

| morass — swamp |

directions. I had met my match. I had been overwhelmed. Alcohol was my master.[31]

Step One is *not* a step of surrender, we *must* admit complete defeat. Powerless is absolute, total, complete, and unconditional. We must admit that in and of ourselves we are without the needed power to recover.

Bill Wilson received the first of the three pieces of information necessary to recover from alcoholism from Dr. Silkworth at Towns Hospital.

Best of all, I met a kind doctor who explained that though certainly selfish and foolish, I had been seriously ill, bodily and mentally.[32]

Bill knew what his problem was, what it meant to be alcoholic. Bill knew he could not drink again because it would be insane for him to do so. And yet, against every reason and desire to stop, he continued to pick up the first drink.

He was powerless to stop once he started and he was powerless to stop starting. He was insane in the area of the first drink and apart from a miracle was doomed to die an alcoholic death.

My weary and despairing wife was informed that it would all end with heart failure during delirium tremens, or I would develop a wet brain, perhaps within a year. She would soon have to give me over to the undertaker or the asylum.

They did not need to tell me. I knew, and almost welcomed the idea.[33]

Suicide in Slow Motion

As a teenager, I was moved to a small town in Southwest Missouri from the big city. I was an above-average student. And being the "new kid," I just wanted to fit in with the so-called "popular" crowd that I watched walking the halls of that new school in such a cool way.

Within weeks of the moving, I had gotten a job and was hooking up with new people who were linked to this popular crowd that I wanted to be part of. They partied all the time, smoking pot and drinking alcohol. I quickly joined them, as it seemed to be the thing to do to be a part of that crowd. I thought that I had found importance. I now had stature, a place where I belonged. *That's it*, I thought, *I have it made.*

It was not long afterward that I found myself dealing the drugs. With this experience, I had discovered what I'd been looking for all along: a sense of being needed and of being important to other people. Drug dealing led to my first arrest at 17. My second came just four weeks later, followed by many, many more.

Those arrests led to requirements that forced me to attend AA meetings and sessions with my first of many substance abuse counselors. Court ordered and completely unwilling, the words that were spoken to me fell on deaf ears. I remember thinking that I just needed to finish out each hour so I could get high.

By the time I was 18, I was being drawn in by methamphetamine and anything else I could get high off of. I couldn't seem to keep from using, no matter what the consequences that I faced were. And obviously, I couldn't stop once I would start.

This life of addiction was all I knew and I couldn't change even when I wanted to. I lasted all of six weeks in college. I watched as the people I ran with changed for the better. I saw others get worse. My family slowly distanced themselves from me. Lost jobs, a broken marriage, and friends who I only wanted to use and who only wanted what they could get out of me.

I had become everything I that I had sworn I would never become. I was able to ease up on my use for a short time, but I could never stop altogether. And sooner or later, it always led to another crash. I just could not stop. I had begun the downhill slope of my addiction, although some times were better than others. I was now living a life of gradual suicide and I knew it.

Ten more miserable years of this life followed, dying a slow death one day at a time. Then one day things changed. My brother was in a program and had come to town for a court date. While there, he and a guy from the recovery ministry that he was living at, looked for me and they found me . . . high and drunk and crazy. They had come to "rescue" me. I did not want to go with them. They literally forced me into the car.

They took me to Branson and introduced me to Church Army. We attended an AA meeting the first evening and the next night went to a worship service. I went high. I soon found myself in detox. There, I committed to the 28-day inpatient treatment program.

My head cleared while in there and upon commencement, I moved into one of the Church Army recovery houses for men. Still full of self and equipped with a major attitude toward everyone, I was evicted for my behavior within a week. They let me come back because of my brother. I knew that I did not want to go back to that old life. But all they were of-fering me was those steps. I gave in. I worked the Common Solution Recovery Program as it was taught to me just three days later.

The results? I have not used drugs or alcohol for almost three years. I have recovered from a seemingly hopeless state of mind and body that is alcoholism and drug addiction. I am married to a beautiful lady with two kids. And I spend most of my time offering others the same solution that I was given. I care about people. I care even more about God. I know that it is only by His grace that I have been reborn.

The life of a slow death is over. I have hope and I have a future. Before I found God through those steps I had neither. I know now that all who seek will find when they truly look with all they are.

"I can't do what ten people tell me to do,
so I guess I'll just remain the same."
— Otis Redding, "Sittin' By the Dock of the Bay"

STEP TWO

WHAT IS *NOT* THE SOLUTION?

*Probably no human resource could have
relieved our alcoholism.*[1]

*The tremendous fact for every one of us is that we have discovered a **common solution**. We have a **way out** on which we can absolutely agree, and upon which we can join in brotherly and harmonious action. This is the great news this book carries for those who suffer from alcoholism.*[2]

Most of us have been offered multiple solutions to the problem of "alcoholism" from many different sources in and out of the rooms of Alcoholics Anonymous. This is the result of the introduction of other programs, especially by treatment centers and other institutions that offer the newcomer therapies and philosophies that directly contradict the message contained in the *Big Book of Alcoholics Anonymous*. Many of these "self-help" viewpoints have filtered into the fellowship of AA and the result is often confusion and a dilution of the fundamental message that alcoholics and addicts were offered as a solution to the problem when the *Big Book* was written and was the program of Alcoholics Anonymous. There are many, many answers being presented to the suffering alcoholic today.

The *Big Book* never presents itself as having the only way to the solution to the problem. It is, however, a way that we are sure from our own experience, works.

We have no desire to convince anyone that there is only one way by which faith can be acquired.[3]

But the *Big Book* very clearly offers only one solution. The directions to find that solution are found in the *Big Book of Alcoholics Anonymous* as they were published in 1939. Chapter Two is titled "There Is **A** Solution." It does not say that there are many or some or a few solutions. There is only the solution that is offered in the text.

There may be others that are effective. However, the *Big Book* offers only one for the simple reason that it worked and continues to work to this day. My sponsor told me that I was perfectly free to work another program if I felt the need whenever I shared the latest "fad" recovery method that I had found. He said, "Go ahead if you want to try it but count me out. I won't be part of any experimenting with your life." He went on to say, "You are a real alcoholic and I only know one way out, the way that worked for me. And that was to work the Twelve Steps in order and in a timely fashion exactly as they are laid out in the *Big Book*."

So, what does the *Big Book* mean when it calls us a "real alcoholic?"

*But what about the **real alcoholic**?*[4]

*The tragic truth that if the man be a **real alcoholic**, the happy day may not arrive. He has lost control. At a certain point in the drinking of every alcoholic, he passes into a state where the most powerful desire to stop drinking is of absolutely no avail. This tragic situation has already arrived in practically every case.*[5]

The real alcoholic has no control over using. He is powerless to stop once he starts and powerless to keep from starting no matter how much he wants to. And by the time he sees the need to stop, he has already passed into a state where his desire will not be enough.

*Most of us have been unwilling to admit we were **real alcoholics**.*[6]

*We know that no **real alcoholic** ever recovers control.*[7]

*Despite all we can say, many who are **real alcoholics** are not going to believe they are in that class.*[8]

*If he is a **real alcoholic** and very far advanced, there is scant chance of success.*[9]

*He agreed he was a **real alcoholic** and in a serious condition.*[10]

So what does it mean to be a "real" alcoholic?

*Moderate drinkers have little trouble giving up liquor entirely if they have a **good reason** for it. They can take it or leave it alone.*
    *Then we have a certain type of hard drinker. He may have the habit badly enough to gradually impair him physically or mentally. It may cause him to die a few years before his time. If a sufficiently **strong reason** — ill health, falling in love, change of environment, or the warning of a doctor — becomes operative, this man can stop or moderate, although he may find it difficult and troublesome and may even need medical attention.*[11]

The moderate drinker has little interest in alcohol. They drink but seldom to excess. These are the drinkers who can control their drinking and are usually drinking as a social activity. And they can stop altogether if they have a *good enough reason* to do so.

The hard drinker drinks a lot like the real alcoholic, sometimes more. His drinking has probably impaired his ability to function and has caused him many problems in his life. The difference between him and the real alcoholic is difficult to distinguish because he gets in the same kind of trouble and drinks heavily as a habit. However, if a *strong enough reason* occurs in his life, he can control the amount that he drinks because he does not have the allergy of the body or he can stop altogether because he does not have the obsession of the mind. He often goes to treatment centers to "dry out" and possibly joins Alcoholics Anonymous. His message is "Don't drink and go to meetings," because that is what worked for him.

But what about the **real alcoholic***? He may start off as a moderate drinker; he may or may not become a continuous hard drinker; but at some stage of his drinking career he begins to lose all control of his liquor consumption, once he starts to drink.*[12]

The real alcoholic is suffering from an **obsession of the mind** that condemns him to drink against his will and an **allergy of the body** that condemns him to death when he does. No reason will be good enough or strong enough to allow the real alcoholic to stop or moderate.

He cannot stop using because of the obsession in his mind and he cannot drink moderately because of the allergy in his body. He is in a position where human aid will not work.

How many of us have many good and even strong reasons not to use again?

"My wife has said that she will leave me if I don't stop."

"The state has threatened to take my kids away from me."

"I will lose my great job."

"I am tired of having no money in the bank."

"The doctor has told me that I could and probably will die if I drink again.

"I am on probation and my PO has said he will send me back to prison if I drop dirty."

These are all good and strong reasons not to use. Now, look back at the last time we drank or used. If we are a real alcoholic and are honest with ourselves, we had those same good and strong reasons before the last time we gave in to the desire. And the time before that? And the time before? And before? As well-meaning and powerful as they were, they did not stop us from using again, did they?

If we are a real alcoholic or a real addict, reasons to "not use" will not stop us from drinking and using again. The obsession will win out sooner or later.

A great example of this truth is found in chapter three of the *Big Book* in the story of Fred the accountant.

I now remembered what my alcoholic friends had told me, how they prophesied that if I had an alcoholic mind, the time and place would come — I would drink again.[13]

> **prophesied —**
> predicted

If we have made the mental conclusion of Step One, we have seen that we are powerless to remove our alcoholic and drug obsession on our own and power is the obvious solution to our problem.

The *Big Book of Alcoholics Anonymous* uses "The Doctor's Opinion" and the first 59½ pages to give us the information required to help us to make the mental conclusions of Steps One and Two.

Our description of the alcoholic (Doctor's Opinion), the chapter to the agnostic (We Agnostics), and our personal adventures before and after (Bill's Story, There Is a Solution, More about Alcoholism) make clear three pertinent ideas:[14]

1. *That we were alcoholic and could not manage our own lives.*
2. *That probably no human power could have relieved our alcoholism.*
3. *That God could and would if He were sought.*

No matter how many reasons we have to not use, no matter what consequences we face, no matter how much we want to stop, we cannot manage to keep from starting. If you are a real alcoholic or addict, then you are drinking and using because you must do it, not because you want to or even need to.

I am convinced personally that alcohol and drugs have kept me from suicide or worse many, many times. Life as I was living it was intolerable and I could face it only with something inside of me to quiet the nerves, to calm the anger; to make my intolerable life tolerable.

> **morals** — principles to live by
> **philosophy** — set of beliefs
> **sufficient** — enough
> **marshaled** — controlled
> **utterly** — totally, completely

If a mere code of morals or better philosophy of life were sufficient to overcome alcoholism, many of us would have recovered long ago. But we found that such codes and philosophies did not save us, no matter how much we tried. We could wish to be moral, we could wish to be philosophically comforted, in fact, we could will these things with all our might, but the needed power wasn't there. Our human resources, as marshaled by the will, were not sufficient; they failed utterly.[15]

So what are human resources? They are simply anything that we can trace back to our own power or to power originating in another person. All self-help programs stem from human resources in some form or other.

Examples of Human Resources

Resolve	Self-help methods
Self-confidence	Isolation
Other drugs	Relationships
Self-knowledge	Physical exercise
Fear	Sponsors
AA meeting attendance	Moving

Good reasons	Professionals
Strong reasons	*Big Book* memorization
Common sense	Scripture memorization
Willpower	Isolation
Memory	New car
Desire to stop	Experimentation
Hospitalization	Psychiatrists
Money problems	Church attendance
Periods of sobriety	Self-control
Necessity	Physicians
Wishes	Self-deception
Getting or losing a job	Code of morals
Fear of losing kids	Intelligence
Treatment centers	Threat of incarceration

*Lack of power, that was our dilemma. We had to find a power by which we could live, and it had to be a **Power greater than ourselves**. Obviously. But where and how were we to find this Power?*

Well, that's exactly what this book is about. Its main object is to enable you to find a Power greater than yourself which will solve your problems.[16]

A real alcoholic is powerless over drugs and alcohol whether he is using them at the moment or not. Powerless is an absolute term. When something is powerless it obviously has no power in it. Not 10 percent power, not 1 percent power, not even .0001 percent. Powerless means 100 percent without power.

Until we are convinced that our human resources, no matter how well-intentioned or good that they are or how much support that they provide, *do not contain the power needed to expel the deadly obsession to use alcohol and drugs, we will continue to rely on them and they will continue to fail us.* And, worst of all, we will never truly admit that we are powerless.

We cannot take Step One as long as we cling to any hope that human resources will work.

We learned that we had to fully concede to our innermost selves that we were alcoholics. This is the first step in recovery.[17]

As long as we are relying on human resources in any form whatsoever, we have not truly taken the first step in recovery. We have never honestly seen and admitted that we are powerless.

Why? If I am a real alcoholic, I am powerless to keep from using again and when I rely on human resources that have "failed utterly," I have added no power in my search for sobriety and I remain powerless.

Powerless +0+0+0+0+0+0+0+0+0+0+0+0 = still powerless!

Once more: the alcoholic at certain times has no effective mental defense against the first drink. Except in a few rare cases, neither he nor any other human being can provide such a defense. His defense must come from a Higher Power.[18]

Banned From the Barn

At the age of 14, I was sneaking alcohol to school with me and I had already been in trouble with the local cops for drinking. My small town's sheriff warned me that I was heading for trouble if I didn't slow down. But by then I had found methamphetamine and it was love at first high. I knew that I had found the best of both worlds. You see, meth enabled me to drink as much as I wanted and never feel out of control. It was the answer to all of my problems.

It didn't take long for meth to start controlling my life. I found myself planning out my using. How much, how often, what time of the day. I was designing the perfect plan to use and not let it get out of hand while thinking I had some sort of control. I knew then that I couldn't control the amount I used, but knowing did not stop me.

Soon after that my life started spinning out of control. No matter how hard I tried I just couldn't stop getting high. I wanted to stop so badly and I tried to quit for years, but I just couldn't do it. Finally, after some serious legal problems, I ended up in a 28-day inpatient treatment center. That's where my life started to change.

While I was in treatment I was introduced to the Twelve Steps of Alcoholics Anonymous in a way I'd never seen. They were explained to me through a program that laid the steps out for me to better understand them. They called the program "Common Solution Recovery." I learned that I had an obsession of the mind coupled with an allergy of my body that condemned me to drink and use. Then I learned that there was a solution to the problem and that solution was God. I struggled with that to say the least. I had turned my back on God because I felt that He had turned His back on me. But my new friends told me I could choose my own conception of God. And not only could I choose my own idea of God and who He was, all I needed to do was be willing to believe in Him. They explained that I wasn't surrendering to God or anyone else at this point. All I needed to do was be willing to believe there was a Power Greater than Myself that could solve my problem. Wow … what a concept! No one had ever given me real hope before. I began to cling to that new feeling.

After watching everyone's lives around me begin to to change and see the glow come from them, I realized that making that decision in Step Three didn't mean anything unless I took some action. So I started on a personal inventory and wrote down my resentments, fears, and how I hurt people with my sex conduct like they told me to. I continued to work those steps the way they told me to and something happened.

What a ride that was and has continued to be every day of my life for over five years. The promises they read at meetings are no longer just words on a page . . . they have actually come true in my life.

My past is not something I regret any longer; I treasure it and thrive on the opportunity to share it to help someone else. God began His work in me and I was in awe at all He was doing. I quickly began working with others and presenting the steps to newcomers. When I worked with another alcoholic/addict and they "got it," it was better than the high I chased for years and I was able to experience it over and over again and it just keeps getting better.

God is truly doing for me what I could never do for myself. He has restored and continues to strengthen my relationship with my family. While I was in my addiction, my mom wouldn't even let me sleep in her barn. After seeing the change in my life from the Common Solution Recovery Program helping me to work the Twelve Steps and to be in relationship with God, she not only let's me stay at her house when I visit, but she offered me her boat and camper when I went on vacation.

He has blessed me with a wonderful man whom I'm now married to. It's amazing at how God works in my life when I stay out of the way. But I even have to do that with His help, because on my own power I'm always making my own decisions and running my life the way I think it should be, not as He wants it to be. Through the amends process I've been able to repair my credit and now God has opened doors for my husband and I to be able to buy our own home. Now I know that's God . . . there's no other way that could've happened.

When the solution is simple,
God is answering.
— Albert Einstein

STEP TWO

WHAT IS THE SOLUTION?

*It was only a matter of being willing to believe
in a Power greater than myself. Nothing more
was required of me to make my beginning.*[1]

*In the preceding chapters you have learned something of alcoholism. We hope you have made clear the distinction between the alcoholic and the non-alcoholic. If, when you honestly want to, you find you cannot quit entirely, or if when drinking, you have little control over the amount you take, you are probably alcoholic. If that be the case, you may be suffering from an illness which **only a spiritual experience** will conquer.*[2]

Two questions. Not 44, not 120. Simply two. That is what the program of recovery in the *Big Book* asks us to answer.

If you cannot quit entirely, if you cannot stop starting, you may have the obsession of the mind. And if you lose control of the amount you consume once you start, you may have the allergy of the body. You are then probably an alcoholic or an addict.

The insidiousness of alcoholism requires that we make a self-diagnosis using our own mind where the obsession (always a lie) resides.

If you are still not convinced that you have this problem, the *Big Book* suggests that you try some controlled drinking.

We do not like to pronounce any individual as alcoholic, but you can quickly diagnose yourself. Step over to the nearest barroom and try some controlled drinking. Try to drink and stop abruptly. Try it more than once. It will not take long for you to decide, if you are honest with yourself about it. It may be worth a bad case of the jitters if you get a full knowledge of your condition.[3]

If I am a real alcoholic, I must diagnose myself. The first step is to admit that I am hopeless because I have no power over alcohol whether I am using or not. One hundred percent self-diagnosis is required and is vital to recovery. If I have investigated the facts of my own life, have looked at the cycle of addiction and still am not convinced of my problem, the experience of the first hundred men and women tells us to go drink.

Note: The *Book* says "walk," not drive, to the bar. Have a couple of drinks and stop if you can. Try it again. Conviction of our condition is worth the withdrawal complications. If this experiment convicts us of our problem, we will then be open to the solution that is offered and be willing to take the action required.

If we don't believe that we have the problem we will never make the effort needed to seek the solution.

If we are planning to stop drinking, there must be no reservation of any kind, nor any lurking notion that someday we will be immune to alcohol.[4]

> **reservation —** reluctance
> **notion —** idea lying in the back of our mind
> **moral —** honest

If I make the first mental conclusion necessary required to recover — "what the problem is" — then I will automatically be in a position to make a second mental conclusion — "what the solution is."

The solution to the problem of alcoholism or any other addiction, as presented in the program of Alcoholics

Anonymous, is a spiritual awakening and a life led on spiritual principles. It is the only solution offered in the *Big Book*.

Well, that's exactly what this book is about. Its main objective is to enable you to find a Power greater than yourself which will solve your problem. That means that we have written a book which we believe to be spiritual as well as moral. And it means, of course, that we are going to talk about God.[5]

Hopefully, we have already concluded that "human resources" were not the answer. We have tried them and they have repeatedly failed.

We have no desire to convince anyone that there is only one way by which faith can be acquired.[6]

The *Big Book of Alcoholics Anonymous* is a book written by people who had a common problem and had found a common solution and were moved to share their experiences with others who suffered.

Each individual, in the personal stories, describes in his own language and from his own point of view the way he established his **relationship with God.**[7]

In our personal stories you will find a wide variation in the way each teller approaches and conceives of the Power which is greater than himself. Whether we agree with a particular approach or conception seems to make little difference. Experience has taught us that these are matters about which, for our purpose, we need not be worried. They are questions for each individual to settle for himself.[8]

There is no demand in the program that everyone have the same conception of God. There is no "God of Alcoholics Anonymous." Each person's conception comes from where he or she is in their life. The person who has been living in the world of drugs and alcohol will probably have a different idea about God than the person who has never had a substance abuse problem. The only requirement is that we are willing to believe that there is a Power greater than ourselves who can remove the obsession to drink and replace it with the truth in the area of the first drink or drug.

There is only one solution offered in the *Big Book*. That solution can never appear to be any better than my understanding of the problem. If I have truly taken Step One, if I have given up on the idea that human resources will solve my problem, then I am open to the possibility that God can solve my problem and I can recover.

The thing that the *Big Book* does not do is compromise the fact that God and God alone is the solution to our problem. Many names for God are used in the text to help anyone with the problem be open-minded to the solution but never in its pages are any other solutions offered or suggested.

On one proposition, however, these men and women are strikingly agreed. Every one of them has gained access to, and believes in, a Power greater than himself or herself. This Power has in each case accomplished the miraculous, the humanly impossible.[9]

This is where problems arise with many who are agnostic or atheist in their beliefs. An *agnostic* is a doubter who claims that they cannot have true knowledge about the existence of God, but does not necessarily deny that God does exist. The *atheist* is the person who denies the existence of God altogether. Both can recover if they are only willing to believe that there may be a Power greater than themselves who can solve their problem.

To one who feels he is an atheist or agnostic, such an experience seems impossible, but to continue as he is means disaster, especially if he is an alcoholic of the hopeless variety. To be doomed to an alcoholic death or to live on a spiritual basis are not always easy alternatives to face.[10]

Step Two says nothing about believing in God. If belief in God were enough, the *Big Book* would be a two-step program. The program of Alcoholics Anonymous says that we must move from where we are now living into an experience of God. We must "come to believe."

We only need to be willing to believe that God can remove the obsession from our life and enable us to live free of the deadly dependency on alcohol and drugs. And, in most cases, the willingness to believe will only come from the knowledge of the depth and weight of our problem.

We needed to ask ourselves but one short question. "Do I now be-lieve, or am I even willing to believe, that there is a power greater than myself?"[11]

If the answer is yes, we have then taken Step Two. We have made the second mental conclusion required to proceed with the program. From the moment that we are willing to believe that God will do for us what we are powerless to do on our own, we are seeking a spiritual experience.

WHAT IS A SPIRITUAL EXPERIENCE?

When the *Big Book* was first published in 1939, the first printing used the term "spiritual experience" many times and gave the reader the impression that the solution was to be sud-den and exciting. The term was replaced in many places with "spiritual awakening" to make the solution more understand-able. A section was added to the book that today is known as Appendix II to explain what is meant by having a spiritual experience or awakening.

Spiritual Experience

*The terms "spiritual experience" and "spiritual awakening" are used many times in this book which, upon careful reading, shows that the personality **change** sufficient to bring about recovery from*

sufficient — adequate	
manifested — made visible	
erroneous — wrong	
transformations — changes	
profound — deep	
alteration — change	

alcoholism has manifested itself among us in many different forms.

*Yet it is true that our first printing gave many readers the impression that these personality **changes**, or religious experiences, must be in the nature of sudden and spectacular **upheavals**. Happily for everyone, this conclusion is erroneous.*

*In the first few chapters a number of sudden revolutionary **changes** are described. Though it was not our intention to create such an impression, many alcoholics have nevertheless concluded that in order to recover they must acquire an immediate and over-whelming "God-consciousness" followed at once by a vast **change** in feeling and outlook.*

*Among our rapidly growing membership of thousands of alcoholics such **transformations**, though frequent, are by no means the rule. Most of our experiences are what the psychologist William James calls the "educational variety" because they develop slowly over a period of time. Quite often friends of the newcomer are aware of the difference long before he is himself. He finally realizes that he has undergone a profound **alteration** in his reaction to life; that such a **change** could hardly have been brought about by himself alone. What often takes place in a few months could seldom have been accomplished by years of self-discipline. With few exceptions our members find that they have tapped an unsuspected inner resource which they presently identify with their own conception of a Power greater than themselves.*

conception — idea	
essence — core	
God-consciousness — awareness	
emphatically — vigorously	

Most of us think this awareness of a Power greater than ourselves is the essence of a spiritual experience. Our more religious members call it "God-consciousness."

Most emphatically we wish to say that any alcoholic capable of honestly facing his problems in the light of our experience can recover provided he does not close his mind to all spiritual

concepts — ideas
intolerance — narrow-minded
belligerent — argumentative
denial — rejection
indispensable — necessary

concepts. He can only be defeated by an attitude of intolerance or belligerent denial.

We find that no one need have difficulty with the spirituality of the program. **Willingness, honesty and open mindedness are the essentials of recovery. But these are indispensable.**[12]

There is a principle which is a bar against all information, which is proof against all arguments and which cannot fail to keep a man in everlasting ignorance — that principle is contempt prior to investigation.[13]
— *Herbert Spencer*

Notice the word "change" and other words meaning "to change" throughout this section. The solution obviously calls for change and the problem prevents me from changing myself or being changed by other programs that rely upon human resources to do so. The *Big Book* offers a changed life resulting from a spiritual awakening as the only solution to the problem of alcoholism.

If you are as seriously alcoholic as we were, we believe there is no middle-of-the-road solution. We were in a position where life was becoming impossible, and if we had passed into the region from which there is no return through human aid, we had but two alterna-

alternatives — choices
intolerable — unbearable

tives: one was to go on to the bitter end, blotting out the consciousness of our intolerable situation as best we could; and the other, to accept spiritual help. This we did because we honestly wanted to, and were willing to make the effort.[14]

Step One is a mental conclusion of our problem.

We admitted that we were powerless over alcohol — that our lives had become unmanageable.[15]

Step Two is a mental conclusion of a possible solution to our problem.

Came to believe that a Power greater than ourselves could restore us to sanity.[16]

Again, we need only to be willing to believe to take Step Two.

*We needed to ask ourselves but one short question: "Do I now believe, or am I even **willing to believe**, that there is a Power greater than myself?" As soon as a man can say that he does believe, or is willing to believe, we emphatically assure him that he is on his way. It has been repeatedly proven among us that upon this simple cornerstone a wonderfully effective spiritual structure can be built.*[17]

The mental conclusion of Step Two requires only a willingness to believe that a Power greater than myself could be the solution to my problem. Nothing more is required.

The newcomer need not believe in anything. Nevertheless, he or she must, at the very least, be willing to believe that there is a Power greater than him or herself which can enter into their life and expel the deadly obsession from their mind (restore them to sanity in the area of the first drink or drug use).

Bill's Story offers an example of willingness and open-mindedness being all that is needed to get started toward recovery.

Bill was drinking alone in his house when his friend and old drinking partner Ebby Thacher came to visit and share with Bill a solution that he had found for his own alcoholism. He told Bill of a simple religious idea and a practical program of action that had worked for him. He had come to share with Bill his own recovery experience.

Bill remained close-minded toward his friend's words and ideas despite what he heard and the obvious changes that he saw in his friend. Rather than continue to argue with Bill about God and religion, Bill's Story (chapter one of *Big Book*) tells us that Ebby offered Bill an alternative.

He said, **"Why don't you choose your own conception of God?"**[18]

Bill took the second step in recovery. He was simply willing to believe that there was a Power greater than himself.

It was only a matter of being willing to believe in a Power greater than myself. Nothing more was required of me to make my beginning. I saw that growth could start from that point. Upon a foundation of complete willingness I might build what I saw in my friend. Would I have it? Of course I would![19]

The basis of success or failure of the program is our willingness to believe that there is a Power greater than ourselves which will solve our problem.

The willingness to believe comes from knowing the depth and weight of our problem as defined in the Doctor's Opinion.

I Am Done With You

It was my third attempt at treatment for my drug problem but the first time without a court order. I had spent over 25 years trying to manage and control my drug use and had failed. I was 47 years old and had been using intravenous drugs pretty much continually. My wife had drawn many lines that I had continually crossed and she finally had told me to get out. She said "Leave now. I am done with you." And this time I knew that she meant it.

I had twice before lost everything in my life and did not know if I could do it again without blowing my head off. The future was bleak.

I called a counselor from seven years earlier and she found me a bed in a local treatment center. While there, I worked the steps as someone who had come in there sharing the Common Solution Program from Church Army told me to do. I was desperate and willing and hopeless, but in less than three weeks I realized that something had happened.

I can't tell you what it was but I can tell you that I felt light and free and forgiven. I wasn't even thinking about using. It had been 25 years since that had happened. I suddenly felt that a new life was possible with God. The self-delusion that I had been living began to slip away. I began to see my faults and shortcomings in the smallest of things.

I was allowed to return to my home after treatment. I had told my wife many times before that I was done with the life so she was skeptical to say the least. But she told me later that she saw something had changed besides my words. She let me back in the house. We stayed married to give it another try.

Because of all the lying and cheating and stealing that I had done in the past she told me that she could not forgive me. I was recovered and home for about a month when she said to me that if we were to have any chance of a life together that she would have to work those steps like I had done. And she did.

That was three years ago and life for us has never been better. God has restored and recreated our marriage. We are happy and free of the hatreds and suspicions that were so much a part of our life before. She even trusts me enough to let me have one of our credit cards to carry for the first time in years. The business that we owned that was once failing is now flourishing. God is truly doing for us what we could never do for ourselves no matter how hard we tried.

I thank the Common Solution Recovery Program and the Twelve Steps for what they have done in my life. But I give God all the credit for what He has done with my life.

Change is the essence of life.
Be willing to surrender what
you are for what you could become.
— Anonymous

STEP THREE

DECISION

*Being convinced, we were at Step Three, which
is that we decided to turn our will and our life
over to God as we understood Him.*[1]

We have been given the information that is essential in making the two mental conclusions to begin the process of recovery contained in the Twelve Steps. We have identified our problem as powerlessness, the first mental conclusion, and followed it with a second mental conclusion of a solution, a power greater than ourselves.

We have taken no action, but this information has placed us in a position that we must make a decision to seek the solution offered or to choose another way. There may be other ways, but, as we have been shown, the *Big Book* offers only one.

These two mental conclusions are reviewed one more time before we proceed.

Our description of the alcoholic (Doctor's Opinion), *the chapter to the agnostic* (Chapter Four), *and our personal adventures before and after* (Chapters One, Two and Three) *make clear three pertinent ideas:*

clear — obvious, plain
pertinent — relevant, important

> *(a) That we were alcoholic and could not manage our own lives.*

This is STEP ONE — *We were powerless over alcohol and our lives had become unmanageable.*

> *(b) That probably no human power could have relieved our alcoholism.*
> *(c) That God could and would if He were sought.*[2]

And STEP TWO — *Came to believe that a Power greater than ourselves could restore us to sanity.*

The Doctor's Opinion and the first 59 ½ pages of the *Big Book* had to contain all the information required to make the two mental conclusions of Steps One and Two when it was published in 1939. There were no meetings that could be attended or sponsors that could be called. The book that contained the instructions to recover had to offer all the information needed to succeed.

The original manuscript, prior to editing of the first edition of the *Big Book* stated the importance of Steps One and Two very clearly. The manuscript as it was written before its final revision:

> If you are not convinced on these vital issues, you ought to re-read the book to this point or else throw it away![3]

Without a complete identification of the problem and a second mental conclusion of a solution that offers hope, we will probably never become interested in working toward the solution that has been identified.

Although there is no recovery in Steps One and Two, they are absolutely vital in making the decision to take action. All the information in The Doctor's Opinion and the first four chapters were written to enable and assist the sufferer to make the conclusions of the problem and the solution.

Every problem solving method requires these two pieces of information to be successful.

Businessman Charles Kettering once stated that a problem well stated is a problem half-solved.

Albert Einstein is quoted as having said that if he had one hour to save the world he would spend *fifty-five minutes defining the problem and only five minutes finding the solution.*

If I have truly seen the depth and weight of my problem and have concluded that apart from God I am hopeless, then I have been placed in a position where I must make a decision.

Being convinced (of these three pertinent ideas), **we were at Step Three**, *which is that we decided to turn our will and our life over to God as we understood Him. Just what do we mean by that and just what do we do?*[4]

First, what do we mean by turning our will and lives over to the care of God?

The first requirement is that we be convinced that any life run on self-will can hardly be a success.[5]

What is self-will? The will is the part of the mind with which someone consciously decides things. It is what we use when we desire things to happen. It is our thinking. And there are only two kinds of will in the world: each person's individual will based on what he or she desires or God's will.

When our lives are being run entirely on our own will we will always be in conflict with others because they are naturally running their own lives based on what they desire. The two individuals' wills will constantly be in conflict with each other and usually with God's will. The results of lives run on self-will, regardless of the motive, will be chaotic and messy.

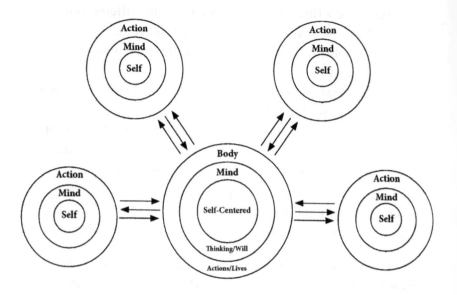

An individual's life run on self-will results in jealousy, resentment, dishonesty, self-pity, indignation, hurt feelings, and so on.

All lives are three dimensional, meaning that everyone is made up of a spirit, a mind, and a body. The spirit (our center), controls how we think (our will), and our thinking will direct our body in the actions that it takes (our lives). As long as self controls our wills, we will remain in conflict with others who are doing the same.

Selfishness — self-centeredness! That, we think, is the root of our troubles.[6]

When we rely on self-will to control our thinking, the results are constant problems in our own lives. We have to make all of our decisions based on emotions such as fear, self-pity, self-delusion, and self-centeredness, and as a result we are continually in conflict with others. These conflicts will result in more resentment, more fear, and more guilt over the actions that we have taken and the harms we have done.

And to overcome the failure and misery that a self-run life is certain to result in, we turn to drugs and alcohol in an attempt to change the way that we feel. And because we have a body that cannot control these substances, this self-centered and selfish thinking will result in an alcoholic/addict's death.

Above everything, we alcoholics must be rid of this selfishness. We must, or it kills us![7]

As we have seen, the main problem of the alcoholic centers in his mind.[8] This is the obsession. The root of our troubles is selfishness and self-centeredness. We can conclude, therefore, that the root of our obsession is selfishness and self-centeredness.

The person with self-will in control will constantly be in conflict with the world and those about him, resulting in the emotional state that forces us to use against all reason and better judgment.

Above everything, we alcoholics must be rid of this selfishness. We must, or it kills us! God makes that possible. And there often seems no way of entirely getting rid of self without His aid. We had to have God's help.[9]

Self-will is a powerful force. Our very lives have been based on it. It is the force that has given us the drive for success in our relationships and in our finances, as well as focused our energy on seeking to be important in society. We have always run our lives based on this self-will and we cannot be rid of it even though we may be able to now see that it is destroying us. We cannot wish it away or decide to remove it ourselves. Only God's will can overcome self-will.

Our decision must be to allow God to take control of our thinking and our actions. This can be done through the working of the Twelve Steps that will allow God to remove the self-will that is blocking us from Him and allow Him to run our lives.

This is the answer to "Just what do we mean by that…"[10]

Now, "just what do we do?"[11]

We now take Step Three. We make the decision to quit playing God by striving to run our own lives and the lives of those around us. Step Three is simply making the choice to take the action that the Program calls for.

Step Three is a decision to seek the solution offered from working the Steps; a decision that places us directly on the path to recovery.

Before we make this important decision, it is suggested that we say a prayer like the Third-Step Prayer in the *Big Book*.

God, I offer myself to Thee — to build with me and do with me as Thou wilt. Relieve me of the bondage of self, that I may better do Thy will. Take away my difficulties, that victory over them may bear witness to those I would help of Thy Power, Thy Love and Thy Way of life. May I do Thy will always![12]

Notice that there is no "Amen" at the end of the prayer. This prayer is the beginning of our recovery, the beginning of our new life, the beginning of our search for the solution to our problem. It is not the end of anything. It is only a decision, and *nothing changes until we take the action called for*.

We are praying for God to remove the deadly obsession and it's root of self with the end in mind to offer to help others to do the same.

Bear in mind that Step Three is only a decision to take action and once again only the beginning of the recovery process. The *Big Book* warns us not to relax or let-up after Step Three.

Therefore the main PROBLEM of the alcoholic centers in his mind.[13]

The obsession centers in the mind.

Selfishness — self-centeredness. That we think is the root of our TROUBLES.[14]

The root of the obsession is selfishness.

Take away my DIFFICULTIES, that victory over them may bear witness to those I would help.[15]

We ask God to remove our obsession so we can help others.

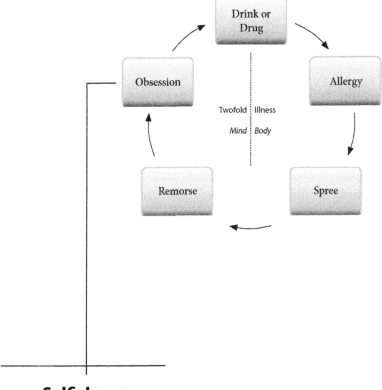

**Selfishness
Self-Centeredness**

This was only a beginning, though if honestly and humbly made, an effect, sometimes a very great one, was felt at once.[16]

Many treatment facilities and other programs offer the first three steps in some form or another and oftentimes the alcoholic or addict feels that they have accomplished something in "working" these steps. But Steps One, Two, and Three as presented in the Program of Alcoholics Anonymous are simply two mental conclusions followed by a decision.

Once again . . . THERE IS ABSOLUTELY NO PERMANENT RECOVERY IN WORKING THE FIRST THREE STEPS OF ALCHOLICS ANONYMOUS AS PRESENTED IN THE *BIG BOOK* INSTRUCTIONS!

For example; if you have broken your arm, you would more than likely easily diagnose your problem, "My arm is broken" — first mental conclusion made.

"I need to go to the emergency room" would likely be your second mental conclusion — the solution identified.

Then you would decide to go to the hospital to experience the solution, especially if you were in great pain.

At this point you have worked the first three steps of the simple problem-solving method that the *Big Book* uses, and nothing would have changed. You would still have a broken arm and would still be exactly in the spot where you started. No relief from the pain of your broken arm would occur until you took the action required to seek the solution. Your decision did not solve anything.

Nothing changes until we take the action to seek the solution that we are willing to believe will solve our problem.

A perfect example of the "1-2-3 Drink" syndrome is found in the *Big Book* in the story of "Jim the Car Salesman."

Our first example is a friend we shall call Jim. This man has a charming wife and family. He inherited a lucrative automobile agency. He had a commendable war record. He is a good salesman. Everybody likes him. He is an intelligent man, normal so far as we can see, except for a nervous disposition. He did no drinking until he was thirty-five. In a few years he became so violent when intoxicated that he had to be committed. On leaving the asylum he came into contact with us.

We told him what we knew of alcoholism and the answer we had found. He made a beginning. His family was reassembled, and he began to work as a salesman for the business he had lost through drinking. All went well for a time, but he failed to enlarge his spiritual life.[17]

Jim was given all the information required to make the mental conclusions of Steps One and Two and he had made the decision of Step Three. He had made a beginning. But he had only made a decision and had not taken the action needed to grow in his relationship with God and he used again.

For if the alcoholic failed to perfect and enlarge his spiritual life through work and self-sacrifice for others, he could not survive the certain trials and low spots ahead. If he did not work, he would surely drink again, and if he drank, he would surely die. Then faith would be dead indeed. With us it is just like that.[18]

Once again, Step Three is a crucial decision and one that must be made to recover and to survive. But we must not stop there. As long as our mind is in possession of the deadly obsession to use, the next drink or drug is just around the corner and we will use against our will sooner or later. Step Three is only a decision and without action, nothing is changed.

This was only a beginning*, though if honestly and humbly made, an effect, sometimes a very great one, was felt at once.*[19]

Jim, like so many of us, had taken the first three steps of the program but no action. He had failed to grow in his spiritual walk and the results were tragic. The obsession remained in control and Jim used again and again until being readmitted to the asylum.

To make a decision without taking action equals good intention but no change results.

Answered Prayers

My life had always been one of self-fulfillment. My earliest memories are about what I wanted. That thought always came first and continued into my adult years. I have always had something in me that told me to live life to the fullest, which I took to mean to live a life that made me feel good when I wanted to and to hell with anyone else and what they wanted. I had no trouble fighting and stepping on others to get what I wanted when I wanted it. But every time I got what I wanted, it soon left me feeling empty and bored and looking for more.

That discontented feeling led me to alcohol and drugs as a way of life. Even when I was happy with my life, it was never quite enough. The drug and drink made me feel even better and when I was sad or unhappy, they helped to get rid of my pain. This insane life soon led to the total dysfunction of my self-centered world. Bills never got paid, relationships and marriages crashed, and I moved all the time hoping to escape the mess of my past.

Jobs, men, and my sanity never lasted for long. One day, my door was kicked in by a drug enforcement team and I was arrested on multiple drug charges. My two daughters were taken from me, my car was repossessed, and I knew that the end of me was near. I was hopeless and helpless to change or fix anything, especially myself. My wonderful parents were sick as they saw their daughter taken to jail. They deserved so much better; so did my girls. But I had no idea what to do or where to go.

I had always believed in God, but to me He was always far away and I never, ever prayed until I had run out of all other options. Before I even got arrested, I knew that my life had to change and I knew I couldn't do it myself. I desperately asked God to help me and I know now He had sent His answer in that drug task force team, though I certainly didn't like it at the time. I have since discovered that God can use anything and anyone to show us that He answers prayer.

The arrest led me to jail. The judge put me in a treatment center where I was introduced to Church Army. They were coming into that place teaching classes on the Twelve Steps of Alcoholics Anonymous. When I got out of treatment the judge allowed me to move into one of their houses as my charges were worked out.

It was there that I found the Common Solution Recovery Program as it was offered at Church Army Branson. They broke down those steps in a way that made sense. God was using that program to show me why I felt so insane at times, why my life was such a disaster.

He convicted me of my selfishness when I started to take the action that they told me to. I began to know God better and He slowly began to restore my life. I learned to face my problems, including my legal and financial ones. I learned to take responsibility for my past and how I had been hurting and using people. I began to attempt to repair the damage that I had caused in making amends to those I had harmed.

Best of all, I learned to pray. Not just when I thought that I needed something but like God was my personal friend. I was discovering that He was just that. I know He is always with me and He stands with me when problems and trials crop up which they invariably do.

By His grace, I got probation instead of prison. By His grace, I got my kids back, with a loving husband thrown in to boot. By His grace, my parents are proud of their daughter now.

Best of all, I am now one of those people who go back to that treatment center and tell people that there is hope in my smile and that there is peace for their lives if they are willing and ready to be changed. I am recovered from that hopeless life and I want everyone to have the same chance that I was given. A chance for a new life that I know now that God has in store for all who surrender to Him.

To look at something as though we had never
seen it requires great courage.
— Henri Matisse

Life is like an onion. You peel it one layer at a
time and sometimes you weep.
— Carl Sandburg

STEP FOUR

THE WRITTEN INVENTORY

I ruthlessly faced my sins. . . .[1]

The Fourth Step of the program of Alcoholics Anonymous
is one of the most talked about and least understood of all of
the Twelve Steps. Part of the reason for this confusion about
this first action step is that there are many varying opinions
about when we should begin to work it.

The *Big Book* clearly states that there is only one option
available to the individual who desires to follow the specific and
exact directions that the text of Alcoholics Anonymous offers.

*NEXT we launched out on a course of vigorous action, the first
step of which is a personal housecleaning, which many of us had
never attempted. Though our decision (Step Three) was a vital
and crucial step, it could have little permanent effect unless AT
ONCE followed by a strenuous effort
to face, and to be rid of, the things in
ourselves which had been blocking us.*

| strenuous — demanding |
| vital — necessary to life |

Our liquor was but a symptom. So we had to get down to causes and conditions.[2]

Alcohol and drugs are symptoms of a deeper fundamental problem in our lives.

Remember the physical symptoms of a hangover? Headaches, nausea, cuts and bruises, shakes, vomiting, diarrhea, and the like are most common. But when the alcohol is out of our system and we have been sober for a few days, these problems clear up.

Now consider the mental problems that accompanied that same hangover. They probably included feelings of anger, restlessness, fear, shame, irritability, discontentment, guilt, and many others. The problem is that when we stop drinking and the alcohol is out of our system the mental problems often get worse and intensify instead of going away.

They tell us that we will feel better if we stop drinking. And we do. The problem is that they mean that we will feel better physically. While that is true, we feel fear and anger more strongly than when we were using; we feel emotions like shame and guilt even more intensely than before!

The problems that led us to drink in the first place are felt deeper and stronger than ever, even to the point of becoming overwhelming. And inevitably, we turn to alcohol and drugs as the solution to the pain that is the result of "thinking" about our problems without the sense of ease and comfort that alcohol and drugs give us. This is what is meant when the book tells us that *"alcohol was but a symptom."*

The Fourth Step is the process that we use to begin to get to the root of our problem. We are seeking to identify what has been blocking us from the relationship with God that we have decided to search fearlessly for. This is the solution to our problem.

We are to begin to take the actions of a personal inventory as soon as we have sincerely made the decision to seek God and allow Him to take control of our will and our lives. Time after time we see many well-intentioned alcoholics and addicts side-tracked by their own or others' thinking that tomorrow would be a better time to start the process. And for many, tomorrow never comes.

Remember, the obsession is still trying to control our thinking and it is cunning, baffling, powerful![3] We have agreed to go to any lengths to recover. If we put off the action that the directions call for, the results will be different than what we have been promised.

If you hesitate at writing your Fourth Step, you are normal. Many will tell you fear is the cause for the delay, and more than likely, it is. But often we see that either you don't believe that you really have the problem or you don't believe that the problem is truly as serious as you have been shown.

If you are a real alcoholic/addict, but believe that you aren't, then the obsession has successfully done its job. If you have an alcoholic mind, the time and place will come that you will use again. Every moment that you delay in writing your Step Four is a decision to try some other method of recovery or, in truth, to not try at all.

Action is necessary to achieve the results desired. Up until now, we have only made the two mental conclusions followed by a decision.

- I have identified my problem and I have been offered a solution.
- I have made the decision to seek the solution that I have been offered.
- But I have taken no action . . . and no action means no change.

Over and over we watch individuals "work" the first three steps of this program, only to be drunk or using a short time later.

The evidence of no change is always "no change."
Once again:

There is ABSOLUTELY NO PERMANENT RE-
COVERY for the real alcoholic or real addict IN work-
ing THE FIRST THREE STEPS OF the program of
ALCOHOLICS ANONYMOUS!

"Wait" is often the door to never. If you have truly seen the
"depth and weight" of your problem, if you have truly taken
Step One, then the willingness to change that is needed will
be there.

But willingness to take the action without actually taking
it is fantasy.

The obsession of the mind will tell you to wait. Well-intentioned persons who have no understanding of the problem or
are suggesting that you work some other program will tell you
to wait. Your own fear will tell you to wait.

"I will do that Fourth Step when . . . I get a job or I find
a place to live or get my wife back or get my car running or
simply when I have more time" are common things that our
obsession tells us.

We ask ourselves, "Why should I bring up all that old
stuff from my miserable past when I am doing so much better
today?"

"Don't rush into something that you don't understand" we
are often told by well-meaning friends and professionals.

The truth is that jobs and houses are not important if you
are in the morgue. Your family will be gone if sobriety is not
found. The "old stuff" from our past is what we have been
using as excuses to use; those are the thoughts that have been
driving us to continue in our old ways. And a clear understanding of this step and, for that matter, any of the others,
will only come after the action of working the step, never
before.

The excuses and reasons may be many but none honestly make sense when compared to the inevitability of returning to that same life that we are so afraid to examine. For the real alcoholic/addict there must be change. And we have seen that the change that is required to recover does not come from any human resource.

The *Book* says that we are taking the action needed to "**face and be rid of**" the things that have kept us separated from God. Step Four is the beginning of facing the truth about ourselves. In Step Five we will expand that search to include God and another human being. In Steps Six and Seven, we will be rid of the things that are blocking us from God's will being done in our lives. To arrive at that point, we must take the called-for action and overcome our fear of the Fourth Step. A willingness to commit to a searching and fearless inventory of our life if is crucial to our survival.

The Bible tells us that "You shall know the truth and the truth will set you free" (John 8:32; New American Standard Bible).

In other words, the Fourth Step is a deliberate effort to identify and face the truth about who and what we really are. It requires action. Anything less means that we have decided to try some other method and the program of Alcoholics Anonymous has been abandoned.

The directions to work the program of recovery of Alcoholics Anonymous are contained in the first 164 pages of the *Big Book*. It is the program that works. And it absolutely requires action on our part.

We have made a mental conclusion that identifies the addiction problem as being a hopeless condition of the mind (obsession) coupled with a hopeless condition of the body (allergy) of which there is no escape through human aid.

We have also mentally identified the solution as a personality change sufficient to recover brought about by a relationship with God or at least are willing to believe this based on what we have witnessed in other recovered addicts and alcoholics.

We have made a decision to seek this vital relationship with God that we are willing to believe is the solution by following the directions to recovery as contained in the text of the *Book of Alcoholics Anonymous*, the first step of action which is Step Four.

Therefore, we started upon a personal inventory. This was Step Four. A business which takes no regular inventory usually goes broke. Taking a commercial inventory is a fact-finding and a fact-facing process. It is an effort to discover the truth about the stock-in-trade.[4]

BUSINESS INVENTORY — PERSONAL INVENTORY

Fact-finding	=	Searching
Fact-finding	=	Fearless
Truth	=	Moral
Stock-in-trade	=	Ourselves

The inventory process is a sincere and honest effort to discover the truth of who we really are and identify how "self" has been blocking us off from the vital personal relationship with God needed for recovery.

Moral is simply another word for truthful. The Fourth Step is a sincere effort to perceive the truth about ourselves. It is not a list of nasty and immoral things from our past. There may be some, even many, but they are not the focus of Step Four.

Actually, we were fooling ourselves, for deep down in every man, woman, and child, is the fundamental idea of God. It may be obscured by calamity, by pomp, by worship of other things, but in some form or other it is there.[5]

> **calamity** — misfortunes
> **pomp** — pride

We finally saw that faith in some kind of God was a part of our make-up, just as much as the feeling we have for a friend. Sometimes we had to search fearlessly, but He was there. He was as much a fact as we were. We found the Great Reality deep down within us. In the last analysis it is only there that He may be found. It was so with us.[6]

So, in order to be recovered, we now must take the action to identify those things that have kept us from the relationship with God that we must find. We need only to follow the directions that are contained in the *Big Book* to do so.

One object is to disclose damaged or unsalable goods, to get rid of them promptly and without regret. If the owner of the business is to be successful, he cannot fool himself about values.

We did exactly the same thing with our lives. We took stock honestly. First, we searched out the flaws in our make-up which caused our failure. Being convinced that self,

flaws — faults
manifestations — appearances

manifested in various ways, was what had defeated us, we considered its common manifestations.[7]

Just as the successful businessman must uncover, discover, and discard the worthless pieces in his business inventory, the alcoholic and addict must undergo the same process in their personal lives. He or she must identify the parts of self that stand in the way of a spiritual awakening and a life led on spiritual principles that are vital to live and to thrive.

If the businessman's store is full of items that no one will buy, he must get rid of them and fill the shelves with sellable products or he will soon go out of business. This sometimes requires difficult choices and will be impossible if he is unwilling to face the truth about what he is selling.

Taking the action of Steps Four and Five is a concerted effort to identify those things that have grown up from our selfishness and self-centered nature and, as a result, are blocking us off from the relationship with God that we must have. In Steps Six and Seven, they will be removed.

A manifestation of self is how selfishness and self-centeredness appear in the physical realm. The three common manifestations of self that we will inventory following the instructions are resentments, fears, and harms done to others in our sexual relationships. Spiritually sick people seem to have these three things in common:

1. They are often filled with anger and are usually living with hate toward someone in their past, whether they know it or not. They are constantly holding a grudge.

2. They live in constant fear of something or someone.

3. They are continually hurting others and themselves in the area of their sex conduct.

Testimony

The Disaster That Was My Life

My first week at Church Army Branson, I attended a class called Common Solution Recovery. They told me that if I followed the instructions that I was given, I would be different; that I could recover from the disaster that was my life.

"Yeah, right," I thought. "What planet did these people come from?" My life had nothing in it but pain and constant struggles. Physical and mental abuse from my parents, and sexual abuse from a neighbor at a very young age was what my life was. Numerous suicide attempts like the one that got me to that place, a life full of drugs of all types, and hustling on the streets. I considered myself hopeless and my life as nothing more than some sort of cosmic joke. And these people were telling me that it could be different.

I wanted to run away, back to my dope buddies, back to trying one more time to fix it myself. All I would need was to score some drugs on credit, sell them, and get a place to live. I had done it before and this time I would do it right and pay back all those people who had hurt me so bad.

I stayed another week and went back to that class for Part Two of the foolishness that they called Common Solution Recovery. This time they started to talk about God and how He would do for me what I couldn't do for myself. I was more shocked than ever and I knew I would run the first chance that I got. I had gotten a job and as soon as I had some money put together, I would be gone.

I knew that God didn't care about me. How many times had I cried out in desperation to Him, only to be ignored?

God did not care and He certainly did not understand me. After all, it was God who allowed me to be hurt and to hurt others all my life.

I stayed another week and I was required to go to that class again. This class was about taking the action of a personal inventory. I was to write down all the people I resented, all the things that I was afraid of, and all the people that I had hurt in my life with my sex conduct. Then I was to talk to someone about all of those horrible things. I went back to the house that night in a rage. Everyone was talking about the class and I exploded and told them that it was all bull----! One of them laughed at me and said he felt the same way at one time. But he told me that he had gone ahead and done what that class taught him and it had worked. He told me that he did it because he knew that he was going to die unless something changed.

I remembered that after my last suicide attempt that I had seen a bright light and felt that I needed to talk to someone about all of the bad things in my life. I had no background in the Bible or in AA and had forgotten all about it. Maybe there was something to this stuff that they were saying.

The next day I talked to that guy and asked him to help me to write and to hear my stuff. I wrote for two days. The pain came pouring out onto that paper and then I met with him. I knew that he would be shocked by what I was going to tell him and I told him so. He laughed and said, "Listen to this," and shared some of his life with me. I knew then that I was not the only crazy person in the world. I relaxed and started talking. We spent hours on my Fifth Step and when we were done I followed the directions of Steps Six and Seven.

I went to bed drained and exhausted but when I woke up I felt a peace like I never knew existed. I will never forget that morning. I felt clean. I felt reborn. I felt that I had a purpose in my life.

I felt and still feel all of those things that I never thought I could. I have a relationship with the God that I thought didn't care. I have experienced things in my life since that day that would have killed me without God. And having a purpose that keeps me going is the same one that kept my friend going when he helped me.

I care for those people I hated, for those people that I thought were lying to me, and especially for those who need the same help that I have been given.

God is indeed doing for me what I could never do for myself!

Resentment is like drinking poison and
waiting for the other person to die.
— Carrie Fisher

STEP FOUR

RESENTMENTS

Resentment is the "number one" offender. It
destroys more alcoholics than anything else.[1]

The first common manifestation of self that the *Big Book* instructs us to examine is in the area of our resentments.

> **Resentment** — Ill feeling of offense, bitterness, or anger caused by a sense of having been badly treated sometime in our past. Resentments are commonly called grudges. Hatred is often the result of resentments.

Resentments are the result of feeling that someone or something in our past has harmed or offended us and are being felt over and over again each time they come to mind. Resentments can also be the result of something that we imagine or know that someone has done, is doing, or is going to do to us.

Resentments enable us to cast the blame for almost any event that has occurred in our lives that we feel has harmed us or those we care about.

Resentments are what we are feeling in the present about an event in our past. We are instructed to inventory the resentments that are happening today, not the events of our past.

Resentments can be and often will be toward ourselves.

Sometimes it was remorse and then we were sore at ourselves.[2]

Resentment is the "number one" offender. It destroys more alcoholics than anything else. From it stem all forms of spiritual disease, for we have not only been mentally and physically ill, we have been spiritually sick. When the spiritual malady is overcome, we straighten out mentally and physically.[3]

> **malady** — illness

We have identified our physical sickness when we admitted to ourselves that we have an allergy of the body and are unable to control our consumption of alcohol or drugs once we have put them into our system. We cannot stop once we start!

We have identified our mental sickness when we admitted to ourselves that we have an obsession of the mind that condemned us to use drugs and drink alcohol against our will and rendered us powerless to keep from doing so again. We could not stop ourselves from starting!

And, finally, we have begun to identify our own spiritual sickness when we started to see that the selfish, self-centered life that we had been living was the origin of all of our troubles, problems, and difficulties; those things that we have seen are the very source of our obsession.

The human resource of medicine cannot fix the allergy of the body of a real alcoholic/addict and human psychiatric treatment cannot remove the mental obsession of a real alcoholic/addict. When God overcomes our selfishness and self-centeredness, the mental and physical problems will be resolved. But to do so, we still must take the action that is called for.

The directions for doing a Fourth Step Inventory of our resentments are found on pages 64–67 of the *Big Book*.

In dealing with resentments, we set them on paper. We listed people, institutions or principles with whom we were angry. We asked ourselves why we were angry. In most cases it was found that our self-esteem, our pocketbooks, our ambitions, our personal relationships (including sex) were hurt or threatened. So we were sore. We were "burned up."[4]

These instructions tell us the following:

That paper and pencil are needed.

> **institutions** — jails, prisons, court systems, schools, churches, treatment centers, etc.
> **principles** — beliefs, traditions, values, ethical standards, etc.
> **self-esteem** — self-worth, pride
> **pocketbooks** — money, possessions
> **ambitions** — desires for the future

That we are to make a list of the people, institutions, and principles that we have resentments toward, going down the paper, top line to the bottom.

In the next column, still going down your paper top to bottom, we are instructed to write down the reason that we have the resentment. What did they do to me that caused me to be resentful toward them?

In the third column, I am to list what part or parts of self are affected by the resentment when I think about what they did to me.

When I re-feel the wrong that I perceive was done to me, I am to identify what part of myself is affected. Is hurt to my self-esteem, my security, my ambitions, or my personal and sexual relationships re-felt when I replay the wrong that was done to me in my mind?

> Self-esteem: Self-esteem is a term used to reflect a person's overall evaluation of him or herself; an appraisal of his or her own worth as perceived high or low.
>
> Security: Security can be emotional (hurt feelings) or financial (dealing with our money, our property, our things that we rely on to feel protected).

Ambitions: My goals, plans, designs for my future; what I want to see happen to me personally.

Personal Relations: My relationships with the other people in my life.

Sex Relations: My relationship with others in the area of my drive for sexual intimacy.

A written inventory is needed to reduce mental and emotional confusion. You are continually thinking about the things that people have done to you anyway, whether you know it or not. Often, people will say that they don't see the sense of digging around in the past. If I am honest with myself, I am already mentally bringing those things up because they give me an excuse to use. They are dominating my thought life and controlling me without my even being aware of it.

Patterns of persons and personal individual shortcomings will soon begin to develop as we look at the truth about ourselves on paper. We can only replay our resentments "one at a time" in our minds. A *Big Book* inventory MUST be written!

NOTE: The inventory form is designed to make the writing process easier to understand and to do. It is not designed to alter the instructions of pages 64–67 and is not required to complete the inventory process. However, the inventory must be written as directed and as definite as the example on page 65.

We went back through our lives. Nothing counted but thoroughness and honesty.[5]

It is vital that we are as thorough and as honest about our past as we can be. We are not striving for perfection. However, we must not intentionally leave anything off of our worksheets regardless of what they may be.

When we were finished we considered it carefully. The first thing apparent was that this world and its people were often quite

Resentment Inventory

Resentment Inventory
Pg 64-67   Big Book

Column I
We listed people, institutions, or principles with whom we were angry.

Column II
We asked ourselves why we were angry?

Column III
What is affected?

- Self Esteem
- Security
- Ambitions
- P-Relations
- S-Relations

After first three Columns are done Turn back to the list in this manner

Column I
Realize that those who harmed you are perhaps spiritually sick.

Column II
What they did are symptoms

Coulmn III
This is the way their sickness hurt you

We pray through every resentment

Prayers
We ask god to save us from being angry

We ask God to help us show them the same tolerance, pity and patience that we would show a sick friend.

Column IV
Now we resolutey look for our own mistakes Where have we been ...

- Selfish
- Dishonest
- Self-Seeking
- Frightened

Resentment Inventory

Resentment Inventory Pg 64-67 Big Book									
Column I We listed people, institutions, or principles with whom we were angry.	**Column II** We asked ourselves why we were angry?	**Column III** What is affected?					**Column IV** Now we resolutley look for our own mistakes. Where have we been …			
		Self Esteem	Security	Ambitions	P-Relations	S-Relations	Selfish	Dishonest	Self-Seeking	Frightened
MR. BROWN										
MRS. JONES										
MY EMPLOYER										
MY WIFE										

After first three Columns are done Turn back to the list in this manner

Column I Realize that those who harmed you are perhaps spiritually sick.

Column II What they did are symptoms

Column III This is the way their sickness hurt you

We pray through every resentment

Prayers
We ask god to save us from being angry

We ask God to help us show them the same tolerance, pity and patience that we would show a sick friend.

Resentment Inventory

Resentment Inventory
Pg 64-67   Big Book

Column I We listed people, institutions, or principles with whom we were angry.	Column II We asked ourselves why we were angry?	Column III What is affected?					After first three Columns are done Turn back to the list in this manner	Column IV Now we resolutey look for our own mistakes Where have we been ...			
		Self Esteem	Security	Ambitions	P-Relations	S-Relations		Selfish	Dishonest	Self-Seeking	Frightened
MR. BROWN	HIS ATTENTION TO MY WIFE										
	TOLD MY WIFE OF MY MISTRESS										
MRS. JONES	MAY GET MY JOB										
	SHE'S A NUT - SNUBBED ME										
	COMMITTED HER HUSBAND, MY FRIEND FOR DRINKING										
MY EMPLOYER	SHE'S A GOSSIP										
	UNREASONABLE										
	UNJUST										
	OVERBEARING										
	THREATENS TO FIRE ME										
MY WIFE	MISUNDERSTANDS AND NAGS										
	LIKES BROWN										
	WANTS HOUSE PUT IN HER NAME										

Instruction band:

Column I Realize that those who harmed you are perhaps spiritually sick.

Column II What they did are symptoms

Coulmn III This is the way their sickness hurt you

We pray through every resentment

Prayers We ask god to save us from being angry

We ask God to help us show them the same tolerance, pity and patience that we would show a sick friend.

Resentment Inventory

Resentment Inventory
Pg 64-67   Big Book

Column I We listed people, institutions, or principles with whom we were angry.	Column II We asked ourselves why we were angry?	Self Esteem	Security	Ambitions	P-Relations	S-Relations	After first three Columns are done Turn back to the list in this manner	Selfish	Dishonest	Self-Seeking	Frightened
MR. BROWN	HIS ATTENTION TO MY WIFE	✓		✓		✓					
	TOLD MY WIFE OF MY MIS-TRESS	✓	✓	✓		✓	**Column I** Realize that those who harmed you are perhaps spiritually sick.				
MRS. JONES	MAY GET MY JOB	✓		✓							
	SHE'S A NUT - SNUBBED ME	✓			✓		**Column II** What they did are symptoms				
	COMMITTED HER HUSBAND, MY FRIEND FOR DRINKING	✓	✓	✓	✓		**Column III** This is the way their sickness hurt you				
	SHE'S A GOSSIP	✓									
MY EMPLOYER	UNREASONABLE	✓	✓				We pray through every resentment				
	UNJUST	✓	✓								
	OVERBEARING	✓	✓				**Prayers** We ask god to save us from being angry				
	THREATENS TO FIRE ME	✓	✓	✓	✓		We ask God to help us show them the same tolerance, pity and patience that we would show a sick friend.				
MY WIFE	MISUNDERSTANDS AND NAGS	✓		✓	✓	✓					
	LIKES BROWN	✓		✓		✓					
	WANTS HOUSE PUT IN HER NAME	✓	✓	✓		✓					

Column III What is affected?

Column IV Now we resolutely look for our own mistakes Where have we been ...

wrong. To conclude that others were wrong was as far as most of us ever got. The usual outcome was that people continued to wrong us and we stayed sore. Sometimes it was remorse and then we were sore at ourselves.[6]

The world and its inhabitants are full of spiritual sickness and these hurting people often hurt others based on their own selfish and self-centered desires. We have identified who they are and what they did to us in the first two columns of the worksheet. That is usually as far as we have gone in the past. We have spent our time taking the inventory of others and we have stayed angry and vengeful at them, often plotting ways to get even.

We should also remain aware that we may have resentments toward ourselves for actions that we have taken in our past that brought harm to ourselves and others.

It is plain that a life which includes deep resentment leads only to futility and unhappiness. To the precise extent that we permit these, do we squander the hours that might have been worthwhile. But

squander — waste
grave — serious, deadly
fatal — deadly
harboring — hanging on to protectively

with the alcoholic, whose hope is the maintenance and growth of a spiritual experience, this business of resentment is infinitely grave. We found that it is fatal. For when harboring such feelings we shut ourselves off from the sunlight of the Spirit. The insanity of alcohol returns and we drink again. And with us, to drink is to die.[7]

Hate and anger will make anyone's life miserable whether they are an alcoholic or not. People waste much of their time reliving and re-feeling the pain that someone or something has caused them in their lives, replaying the experience over and over again.

Resentment blocks off any possible relationship with God because hate is never His will for anyone, including the alcoholic. For the alcoholic, a resentment effectively shuts down our relationship with God and the obsession takes control and we drink or use. And because we cannot control the amount we use because of the allergy of our body, sooner or later it will destroy us.

If we were to live, we had to be free of anger. The grouch and the brainstorm were not for us. They may be the dubious luxury of normal men, but for alcoholics these things are poison.[8]

brainstorm — sudden outburst of temper **dubious** — doubtful

Persistent anger, irritability, and sudden rages are like a death sentence to the alcoholic. These resentments are a sign of a spiritual sickness that non-alcoholics can get away with. Although it is not good for the non-alcoholic, they can hold onto their resentments without experiencing uncontrolled drinking or overdose as a result. The person who is not in possession of the obsession of the mind or the allergy of the body can get angry and stay angry without facing the consequences that an alcoholic or addict does.

But resentment is a certain sign that we are out of a right relationship with God which means that self is in control of our lives. The result is that we are defenseless against the obsession. And when the obsession is in control, we must use. Remember that no reason or thought process can overcome it. And because we are unable to control the amount we drink or use once we start, we will sooner or later die in our addiction.

We turned back to the list, for it held the key to the future. We were prepared to look at it from an entirely different angle. We began to see that the world and its people really dominated us. In that state, the wrong-doing of others, fancied or real, had power to actually kill. How could we escape? We saw that these resentments must be mastered, but how? We saw that we could not wish them away any more than alcohol.[9]

The inventory must be written for us to see in black and white how our own lives have been dominated by our resentments toward people, institutions, and principles from our past.

An event or a wrong need not even have taken place. We can imagine or think that we know the truth about something that someone might have done or is planning to do. This resentment can be just as deadly to a real alcoholic as the resentment that we hold for something that we know has been done. The occurrence need not even to have actually happened for the resentment to be real and deadly.

We have seen the deadly consequences of holding onto resentments. We now see the need to be rid of resentments if we want to live. But we know that we can't just wish them away any more than we can wish away alcohol or self-centeredness. They are very much a part of us, of who we are.

We are powerless to rid ourselves of resentments, so we must turn to God.

This was our course: We realized that the people who wronged us were perhaps spiritually sick. Though we did not like their symptoms and the way these disturbed us, they, like ourselves, were sick too. We asked God to help us show them the same tolerance, pity, and patience that we would cheerfully grant a sick friend. When a person offended we said to ourselves, "This is a sick man. How can I be helpful to him? God save me from being angry. Thy will be done."[10]

realized — had become aware of the possibility

We now look at our resentment list differently. In the first column we have a list of people and institutions made up of human beings. People who, just like us, are spiritually sick, selfish, and self-centered. They have committed selfish acts that have harmed us and others. Column Two lists the symptoms of their selfishness, (the actions that they have taken) and Column Three is how they have affected us and continue to affect us today because we continue to mentally replay them.

We asked God . . . is the beginning of a prayer to help us to display to the offender forgiveness by our actions toward them in His Spirit. We ask God to give us the strength to stop displaying toward them the hate we have felt and, instead to give us the power to show them the same tolerance, patience, and pity we would cheerfully grant a sick friend; the same tolerance and patience that we have been shown by God.

This prayer should be prayed for each person on your resentment list *regardless of who they are or what they have done. Including ourselves.*

We are inventorying our resentments, not what they did to harm us. We have been taking the other person's inventory since the event and all it has done is feed into and worsen our problem. The inventory is of our own resentments as we re-feel them at the present time.

> *NOTE: Many alcoholic men and women have some form of sexual abuse in their background. They feel that they can never forgive the offender. They are correct. In and of ourselves, we will never be able to forgive. However, this person who harmed us must be included on our resentment list.* **We must face this evil or we will use again.** *Regardless of what they did, whether they are alive or not, whether we have "worked through it" or not, they must be included on our list. And we must be willing to ask God to help us. To compromise the program or make anyone on our list an exception is to risk using and death.*

When the thought arises again of the person and the wrong that they have done to us — and it will — we are to continue in prayer for God to protect us from the anger that arises and remember that He is the only power that can free us of our resentments. To refuse to ask God to help us to forgive any one individual is like being stung to death by a single bee.

NOTE: Asking God for the help to forgive the sick person does not mean excusing the consequences of the wrong action that the other person faces.

Praying for God to help us show the offending party tolerance, pity, and patience is all about being in right relationship with God and His will for us. It has nothing to do with our relationship with that other person. Their relationship with God is not our business; it is between God and them.

We must only be willing to ask Him for help. He has all the power that we need.

The Fourth Step is not the amends process; it is an effort to face the things which have been blocking us from God.

We avoid retaliation or argument. We wouldn't treat sick people that way. If we do, we destroy our chance of being helpful. We cannot be helpful to all people, but at least God will show us how to take a kindly and tolerant view of each and every one.[11]

A willingness to forgive sometimes may mean that I have to approach God again and again with what I thought I had already given up. To lack willingness to forgive or to give up our resentment against someone is a natural thing. Yet to be unwilling to do so will keep us blocked off from the relationship with God that we are seeking and locked up in our prison of self. We will return to drink and drugs for the relief from our resentments because we are unwilling to ask God to remove them.

The *Big Book* promises that we cannot be helpful to all the persons on our list but that God will show us how to have a different outlook toward them than we have had in the past.

Referring to our list again, putting out of our minds the wrongs others had done, we resolutely looked for our own mistakes. Where had we been selfish, dishonest, self-seeking,

resolutely —determinedly	
self-seeking — self-centered	

Resentment Inventory

Resentment Inventory — Pg 64-67 Big Book

Column I We listed people, institutions, or principles with whom we were angry.	Column II We asked ourselves why we were angry?	Column III — What is affected?					After first three Columns are done Turn back to the list in this manner	Column IV Now we resolutely look for our own mistakes Where have we been ...			
		Self Esteem	Security	Ambitions	P-Relations	S-Relations		Selfish	Dishonest	Self-Seeking	Frightened
MR. BROWN	HIS ATTENTION TO MY WIFE	✓	✓	✓		✓		✓	✓		✓
	TOLD MY WIFE OF MY MISTRESS	✓	✓	✓		✓		✓			✓
	MAY GET MY JOB	✓	✓	✓				✓			✓
MRS. JONES	SHE'S A NUT - SNUBBED ME	✓		✓	✓		Column I Realize that those who harmed you are perhaps spiritually sick.	✓	✓	✓	✓
	COMMITTED HER HUSBAND, MY FRIEND FOR DRINKING	✓		✓	✓		Column II What they did are symptoms	✓			✓
	SHE'S A GOSSIP	✓			✓		Column III This is the way their sickness hurt you	✓		✓	
MY EMPLOYER	UNREASONABLE	✓	✓		✓		We pray through every resentment	✓		✓	
	UNJUST	✓	✓				Prayers We ask god to save us from being angry	✓			
	OVERBEARING	✓	✓				We ask God to help us show them the same tolerance, pity and patience that we would show a sick friend.	✓	✓		✓
	THREATENS TO FIRE ME	✓	✓	✓				✓		✓	✓
MY WIFE	MISUNDERSTANDS AND NAGS	✓	✓	✓	✓	✓		✓		✓	✓
	LIKES BROWN	✓	✓		✓	✓		✓			✓
	WANTS HOUSE PUT IN HER NAME	✓		✓		✓		✓	✓		✓

Resentment Inventory

Resentment Inventory Pg 64-67 Big Book		Column III What is affected?						Column IV Now we resolutely look for our own mistakes. Where have we been …			
Column I We listed people, institutions, or principles with whom we were angry.	**Column II** We asked ourselves why we were angry?	Self Esteem	Security	Ambitions	P-Relations	S-Relations		Selfish	Dishonest	Self-Seeking	Frightened
PERSON WHO MOLESTED ME	HURT ME WHEN I WAS 5.	✓	✓	✓	✓	✓		✓	✓	✓	✓
MYSELF	NOT STAYING SOBER	✓	✓	✓	✓	✓			✓		✓
	HURTING MY FAMILY	✓	✓	✓	✓			✓	✓		✓
	NOT PAYING CHILD SUPPORT	✓	✓	✓	✓			✓	✓		✓
	GETTING ARRESTED	✓		✓	✓	✓		✓	✓	✓	✓
	NOT FINISHING ANYTHING	✓		✓	✓			✓	✓	✓	
GOD	LETTING MY FATHER DIE							✓	✓		✓
	ALLOWING ME TO BE AN ADDICT					✓		✓	✓		✓

After first three Columns are done Turn back to the list in this manner

Column I
Realize that those who harmed you are perhaps spiritually sick.

Column II
What they did are symptoms

Coulmn III
This is the way their sickness hurt you

We pray through every resentment

Prayers
We ask god to save us from being angry

We ask God to help us show them the same tolerance, pity and patience that we would show a sick friend.

and frightened? Though a situation had not been entirely our fault, we tried to disregard | **disregard** — ignore |
the other person entirely. Where were we to blame? The inventory was ours, not the other man's. When we saw our faults, we listed them. We placed them before us in black and white. We admitted our wrongs honestly and were willing to set these matters straight. [12]

> *NOTE: The worksheet illustrations thus far have come directly from Page 65 of the Big Book. While desiring not to add to the material that the Big Book offers, we have received many requests asking us to add examples of some of the very common and most serious resentments that can keep us separated from God and sick in ourselves. This additional illustration of page 101 includes resentments at God, resentments at ourselves and resentment examples at persons who have molested us sexually.*

The last column of the inventory sheet is the root cause of the resentment. All resentments will stem from our own selfish, dishonest, self-centered, and frightened way of living and thinking! This is where we were to blame. Our own selfish thoughts and self-centered actions are the cause of our resentments. We may have had absolutely no part in causing the other person to harm us. But the resentment itself will always stem from our own selfishness.

Resentments are NOT caused by something that someone else has done to us. They are always caused by our own selfishness and self-centeredness. Without exception, they arise from within us. The origin of our resentment is always our own defects of character, our own shortcomings. This is an inventory of *our* resentments, not the people that we have been blaming for them.

Selfishness, dishonesty, self-seeking and fear are inevitably found to be at the root of our resentments.

The same selfishness that is the root of our obsession!

Therefore the main PROBLEM of the alcoholic centers in his mind.[13]

Selfishness — self-centeredness. That we think is the root of our TROUBLES.[14]

Take away my DIFFICULTIES, that victory over them may bear witness to those I would help.[15]

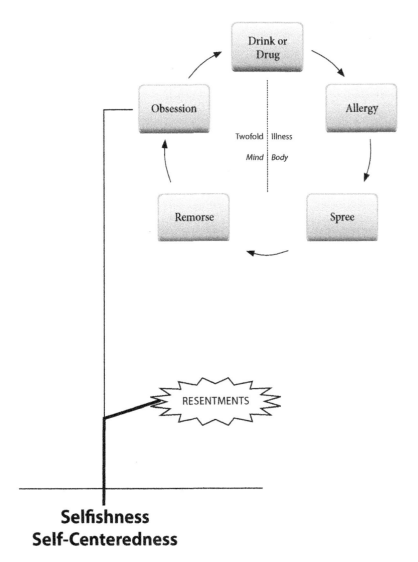

**Selfishness
Self-Centeredness**

I am an old man and I have had many troubles
in my life . . . most of which never happened.
— Mark Twain

STEP FOUR

FEARS

*It was an evil and corroding thread; the fabric
of our existence was shot through with it.*[1]

The second common manifestation of self that we are instructed to inventory is fear. Note that if we have followed
directions we have already inventoried a number of our fears
when we processed our resentments.

*Notice the word "fear" is bracketed alongside the difficulties with
Mr. Brown, Mrs. Jones, the employer, and the wife. (See the inventory example on page 65 of the* Big Book.*) This short word
somehow touches about every aspect of our lives. It was an evil
and corroding thread; the fabric of our existence was shot through
with it. It set in motions trains of circumstances which brought us
misfortune we felt we didn't deserve. But did not we, ourselves, set
the ball rolling? Sometimes we think fear ought to be classed with
stealing. It seems to cause more trouble.*[2]

While taking our resentment inventory, we have seen that
when our ambitions were threatened, fear was part of the root
cause of our resentment. Each time that what I desired for the
future was threatened by what someone had done, I discovered

that fear was the driving force in myself that resulted in my holding onto resentments toward them.

We all have ambitions for our own lives in some area and if we are relying on ourselves to achieve the results that we are wishing for, we will be constantly living in fear of someone or something possibly interfering with our hopes. And, when they interfere with our ambitions, we become angry and resentful. These resentments often lead to retaliation which causes even more fear-based resentment.

This fear robs us of any chance for peace in our own lives or the lives of those around us. We take a look at this truth after we have inventoried our resentments.

Now we are given the instructions to inventory our remaining fears. Again, the Inventory Worksheet is to make the process clearer and easier for us to see the patterns that our selfishness and self-centered way of life has resulted in.

We reviewed our fears thoroughly. We put them on paper even though we had no resentment in connection with them. We asked ourselves why we had them. Wasn't it because self-reliance failed us? Self-reliance was good as far as it went, but it didn't go far enough. Some of us once had great self-confidence, but it didn't fully solve the fear problem, or any other. When it made us cocky, it was worse.[3]

infinite —unlimited
finite — limited
extent — amount
calamity — misfortunes
serenity — peacefulness

Perhaps there is a better way — we think so. For we are now on a different basis; the basis of trusting and relying upon God. We trust infinite God rather than our finite selves. We are in the world to play the role He assigns. Just to the extent that we do as we think He would have us, and humbly rely on Him, does He enable us to match calamity with serenity.[4]

The "different basis" that we are now on is the foundation of relying on and trusting in an all powerful God rather than in our powerless selves. We made the decision to do this in

Fear Inventory

Fear Inventory Pg 68 Big Book			Fear Prayer
Column I What am I afraid of?	Column II Who am I relying on?		
	God	Self	
			Use this prayer for all fears as they crop up. We ask God to REMOVE our fear and DIRECT our attention to what He would have us be.

Fear Inventory

Fear Inventory Pg 68 Big Book Column I What am I afraid of?	Column II Who am I relying on?		Fear Prayer
	God	**Self**	
SOBRIETY			Use this prayer for all fears as they crop up.
DEATH			We ask God to REMOVE our fear and DIRECT our attention to what He would have us be.
RELAPSE			
FAILURE			
SUCCESS			
WIFE LEAVING			
HURTING OTHERS			
LOSING JOB			
PRISON			
BEING POOR			
COMMITMENT			

Fear Inventory

Fear Inventory Pg 68 Big Book			

Fear Inventory

Column I What am I afraid of?	Column II Who am I relying on?		Fear Prayer
	God	**Self**	
SOBRIETY		✓	
DEATH		✓	
RELAPSE		✓	
FAILURE		✓	
SUCCESS		✓	
WIFE LEAVING		✓	
HURTING OTHERS		✓	
LOSING JOB		✓	
PRISON		✓	
BEING POOR		✓	
COMMITMENT		✓	

Use this prayer for all fears as they crop up.

We ask God to REMOVE our fear and DIRECT our attention to what He would have us be.

Step Three. Writing and following the directions of the *Big Book* Step Four Fears Inventory is the action we must take for that decision to become a reality in our lives.

God has all power and we have admitted that we are powerless. His Power is necessary to overcome the self-centered and destructive fears in our lives — the kind of fears that inevitably lead us to make poor decisions and to take wrong action that is certain to lead to disastrous consequences.

> **paradoxically** — the opposite of what we would think
> **verdict of the ages** — result of years of experience
> **courage** — guts
> **commence** — begin

We never apologize to anyone for depending on our Creator. We can laugh at those who think spirituality the way of weakness. Paradoxically, it is the way of strength. The verdict of the ages is that faith means courage. They trust their God. We never apologize for God. Instead, we let Him demonstrate, through us, what He can do. **We ask Him to remove our fear and direct our attention to what He would have us be.** *At once, we commence to outgrow fear.*[5]

Reliance upon God and His power is the foundation for our new way of life. This dependence is likely the opposite of what our out-of-control instincts and years of emotional bad habits have dictated in our lives. We pray this prayer out of a willingness to do so and not necessarily because we believe that it will make any difference. But we must be willing to take this action.

Instead of dreading a future occurrence or plunging into actions based on these fears, the program of Alcoholics Anonymous tells us to pray. We ask God in prayer to remove our fear because fear blocks us from Him and His direction for us. We then ask Him what that direction should be (trusting in and relying upon God).

We have now completed the second part of our inventory of self.

Therefore the main PROBLEM of the alcoholic centers in his mind.[6]

Selfishness — self-centeredness. That we think is the root of our TROUBLES.[7]

Take away my DIFFICULTIES, that victory over them may bear witness to those I would help.[8]

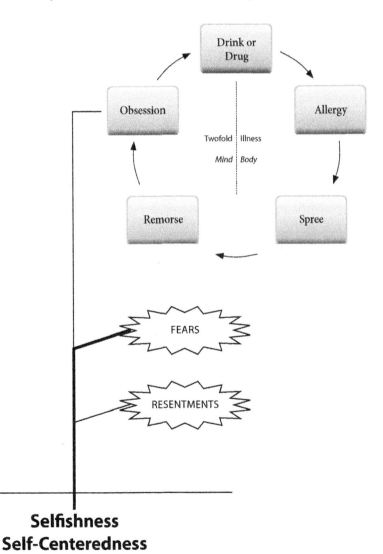

**Selfishness
Self-Centeredness**

I used to make love under a red sunset,
I was making promises I would soon forget.
She was pale as the lace of her wedding gown,
But I left her standing before love came to town.
When love comes to town I'm gonna jump on that train.
When love comes to town I'm gonna catch that flame.
Maybe I was wrong to ever let you down,
But I did what I did before love came to town.
— Bono, U2, "When Love Came to Town"

STEP FOUR

SEX CONDUCT

*Now about sex. Many of us need an overhauling
there. But above all, we tried to be sensible on this
question. It's so easy to get way off track.*[1]

We are beginning to see how selfishness and self-centeredness have been controlling our lives. We now look at our sex conduct and the damage that our own selfish actions have caused ourselves and others in the area of this powerful instinct.

Like our Resentment Inventory and our Fear Inventory, we are seeking the truth about ourselves and we must be as thorough and honest as we can. We must follow the directions that we have been given. But before we begin to write the inventory of our sex conduct, we are given reasons to do so.

Here we find human opinions running to extremes — absurd extremes, perhaps. One set of voices cry that sex is a lust of our

113

overhauling — major repairs
sensible — reasonable
opinions — attitudes
extremes — far-reaching boundaries
lust — desire
procreation — reproduction
bewail — complain about
significance — importance

lower nature, a base necessity of procreation. Then we have the voices who cry for sex and more sex; who bewail the institution of marriage; who think that most of the troubles of the race are traceable to sex causes. They think we do not have enough of it, or that it isn't the right kind. They see its significance everywhere. One school would allow man no flavor for his fare and the other would have us all on a straight pepper diet.[2]

The range of attitudes and beliefs about sex conduct are far reaching in today's society, from ultra-conservative to extremely liberal, from traditional and fundamentalist to radical and tolerant. Both can be exceedingly judgmental toward one another, resulting in hard feelings and heated debates.

We want to stay out of this controversy. We do not want to be the arbiter of anyone's sex conduct. We all have sex problems. We'd hardly be human if we didn't. What can we do about them?[3]

controversy — debate
arbiter — judge
conduct — behavior
unjustifiably — without cause
arouse — provoke
jealousy — resentment
suspicion — distrust
bitterness — hostility

Sex has caused problems in everyone's life. No one has had perfect conduct in the area of this powerful instinct. The inventory is not designed to judge anyone's sex life or to demand that you follow values and rules imposed by others.

The purpose of the Sex Conduct Inventory is to honestly examine how "self" has controlled our conduct and has caused damage to ourselves and to others. We must see the truth of our past to allow for change in our future.

Review of Our Past Conduct

Sex Conduct Inventory Pg 68-70 Big Book							
Column I **Who have I hurt?**	**Column II** **What did I do?** **What should I have done?**	**Column III** **Did I arouse:**			**Column IV** **Was I:**			**Sex Conduct Prayers**
		Jealousy	Suspision	Bitterness	Selfish	Dishonest	Inconsiderable	
								We ask God to mold our ideals and help us to live up to them. We ask God what to do about each specific matter. We pray for the right ideal, guidance, sanity, and for the strength to do the right thing.

The instructions on how to write our Sex Conduct Inventory are now presented.

We reviewed our own conduct over the years past. Where had we been selfish, dishonest, or inconsiderate? Whom had we hurt? Did we unjustifiably arouse jealousy, suspicion, or bitterness? Where were we at fault, what should we have done instead? We got this all down on paper and looked at it.[4]

Each instance of harm caused with our sex conduct should be inventoried. We honestly look at what we did to cause the harm to others and what we should have done instead.

We will quickly see that our selfishness has been the cause of our problems in this area. We may even come to see that being driven by our own selfish desires, the actions that we took were inevitable.

In the same way as resentments and fears we may use the provided form that has been designed to make the process easier to understand and to examine ourselves or we can follow the directions as laid out in this paragraph of the *Big Book*. Again, this worksheet is not designed to change the process but rather to simplify it. However, with either method, the inventory MUST be written. The directions for writing our past sex conduct as the third section of the Fourth Step are found on page 68–70 of the *Big Book*.

We make a list of all the persons we have harmed with our sex conduct in the first column.

> NOTE: The book does not say we make a list of "whom we had slept with" or "who we have had sex relations with." The question that we must answer is, "Who have I harmed?" We have likely harmed many others with our actions while selfishly involved in our sex conduct.

Review of Our Past Conduct

Sex Conduct Inventory
Pg 68-70 Big Book

Column I Who have I hurt?	Column II What did I do? What should I have done?	Column III Did I arouse:			Column IV Was I:			Sex Conduct Prayers
		Jealousy	Suspision	Bitterness	Selfish	Dishonest	Inconsiderable	
MY WIFE	CHEATED ON MY WIFE REMAINED FAITHFUL	✓	✓	✓	✓	✓	✓	We ask God to mold our ideals and help us to live up to them.
MY MISTRESS								
MY CHILDREN								We ask God what to do about each specific matter.
MY MISTRESS KIDS								
HER HUSBAND								We pray for the right ideal, guidance, sanity, and for the strength to do the right thing.
MY BOSS								
OUR FRIENDS								
MY FELLOW WORKERS								

In Column Two, we list what we did wrong (where were we at fault?) and what we should have done instead in each instance.

We answer the question "Did I arouse jealousy, suspicion, or bitterness?" in Column Three.

Next, in the Fourth Column, we look at the source of our sex conduct. Was it our selfishness, our dishonesty, and our inconsiderate thinking? Probably we will see that all three of these shortcomings were involved. We will likely see that self-ishness and self-centeredness have been the driving force in our sex life.

We inventory each action of our past sex conduct that has caused harm to others and to ourselves. Thoroughness is vital to the effectiveness of the inventory process.

In this way we tried to shape a sane and sound ideal for our future sex life. We subjected each relation to this test — was it selfish or not? We asked God to mold our ideals and help us to live up to them. We remembered always that

shape — form
sane — rational
sound – sensible
ideal — model
loathed — hated

our sex powers were God-given and therefore good, neither to be used lightly or selfishly nor to be despised and loathed.[5]

We use this part of the inventory process to examine how our own self-centered desires for control, security, and affection have caused harm to other persons in our lives.

We pray to God for the right thoughts and actions that He would have us live for in our future sex conduct.

make amends — repair the damage

Whatever our ideal turns out to be, we must be willing to grow toward it. We must be willing to make amends where we have done harm, provided we do not bring still more harm in so doing. In other words, we treat sex as we would any other prob-lem. In meditation, we ask God what we should do about each specific matter. The right answer will come, if we want it.[6]

Willingness to change is the key to our new life. I am powerless to change without God's help. Just like resentments and fears, I must ask God to help me to be willing to change. This includes a willingness to make the effort to repair the damage that my selfish conduct of the past has caused, provided I do not cause even more hurt in doing so. I must pray for the knowledge to make the right decisions and to take the right actions.

God alone can judge our sex situation. Counsel with persons is often desirable, but we let God be the final judge. We realize that some people are as fanatical about sex as others are loose. We avoid hysterical thinking or advice.[7]

counsel — guidance
fanatical — obsessed with rules and regulations
loose — unrestrained
hysterical — fanatical

We are coming to realize that God designed and created sex. Therefore, we must allow Him to judge our sex situation. And we must remain willing to grow toward His will for us in this area of our lives.

We can talk it over with others as God directs us to do so, but as we come to depend and rely on God's guidance, we are able to distinguish good advice from bad.

Suppose we fall short of the chosen ideal and stumble? Does this mean we are going to get drunk? Some people tell us so. But this is only a half-truth. It depends on us and our motives. If we are sorry for what we have done and have the honest desire to let God take us to better things, we believe we will have learned our lesson. If we are not sorry, and our conduct continues to harm others, we are quite sure to drink. We are not theorizing. These are facts out of our experience.[8]

theorizing — guessing

As we grow toward our ideal of a God-directed sex life we may make mistakes based on our old selfish nature. If we hurt someone and are sorry for doing so, we ask God to forgive us, to give us the courage and wisdom to make amends, and to direct us to a better way of living. If we are not willing to pray for help and truth in this dangerous area, we are still separated from God and will continue to hurt ourselves and others with our sex conduct.

If we do continue to hurt others and do not have any feelings of remorse, we will remain separated from God and the obsession will lead us back to using alcohol and drugs. Selfishness will continue as the driving force in our lives and the obsession that grows from that same root will drive us to use. These are the experiences of every alcoholic who has seen the truth about himself or herself in this inventory process.

earnestly — sincerely
questionable — uncertain

To sum up about sex: We earnestly pray for the right ideal, for guidance in each questionable situation, for sanity, and for strength to do the right thing. If sex is very troublesome, we throw ourselves the harder into helping others. We think of their needs and work for them. This takes us out of ourselves. It quiets the imperious urge, when to yield would mean heartache.[9]

We will come to rely on God to guide our thinking and direct our actions in the area of our sex conduct the same way as in the other areas of our lives. If sex is a major problem area, we are to unselfishly offer ourselves to work even harder with others who may need our help. We cannot think of others well-being and be working to help them meet those needs and be selfish and self-centered at the same time.

INVENTORY SUMMARY

If we have been thorough about our personal inventory, we have written down a lot. We have listed and analyzed our resentments. We have begun to comprehend their futility

analyzed — examined
comprehend — consider, to figure out as truth
futility — uselessness
fatality — deadly outcome

Therefore the main PROBLEM of the alcoholic centers in his mind.[10]

Selfishness — self-centeredness. That we think is the root of our TROUBLES.[11]

Take away my DIFFICULTIES, that victory over them may bear witness to those I would help.[12]

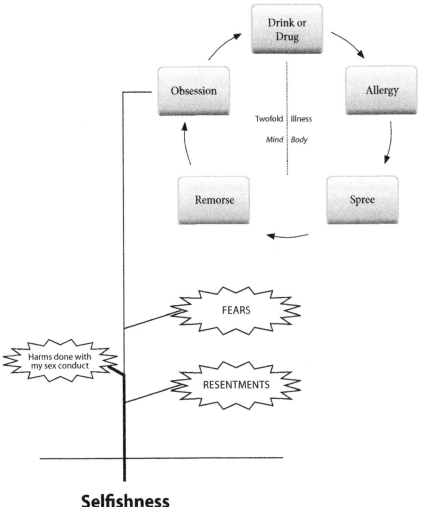

**Selfishness
Self-Centeredness**

commenced — begun
tolerance — acceptance
good will — helpfulness

and fatality. We have commenced to see their terrible destructiveness. We have begun to learn tolerance, patience, and good will toward all men, even our enemies, for we look on them as sick people. We have listed the people we have hurt by our conduct, and are willing to straighten out the past if we can.[13]

These are the promises of working a thorough Step Four. We have written down our inventory and should now be beginning to see the truth about who and what we really are and the selfishness that has been driving our lives. We should be beginning to experience the truth that our life apart from God's direction is doomed.

We will, by now, be starting to experience the results of prayer, possibly for many of us, for the first time. We will begin to experience forgiveness, both the giving and receiving of it. We will begin to find courage to face the future. We will have begun our list of amends.

But there is more action to be taken.

In this book you read again and again that faith did for us what we could not do for ourselves. We hope that you are convinced now that God can remove whatever self-will has blocked you off from Him. If you have already made a decision, and an inventory of your grosser handicaps, you have made a good beginning. That being so, you have swallowed and digested some big chunks of truth about yourself.[14]

The experiences that are beginning — forgiveness, courage, love for others — are not something that we could do in and of ourselves. We are beginning to trust in God and are discovering and experiencing God's power in our lives.

We know now that this freedom from resentments and fear and guilt can only be happening as the result of our willingness to seek God's power for the answer to our problems.

We have decided to do so and have taken the action that the directions called for. We are becoming more and more certain that God will remove whatever interferes with us coming into a vital relationship with Him.

Keep in mind that we have only made a decision to seek Him and have just begun the process to identify what separates us from His needed power.

In Step Three, we made a beginning.[15] Now, having completed Step Four, we have still only made a good beginning.[16]

There is still more action to be taken in our effort to discover what has blocked us off from God.

*In confession . . . we open our lives to healing,
reconciling, restoring and uplifting grace of
Him who loves us in spite of what we are.*
— Louis Cassels

STEP FIVE

DISCUSSING OURSELVES
WITH ANOTHER PERSON

*My schoolmate visited me, and I fully acquainted him
with my problems and deficiencies.[1]*

When we follow directions and take the action as required in Steps Four, Five, Six, and Seven, it is a willing effort on our part to face and to be rid of the things in ourselves which block us from the relationship with God that we are beginning to see that we must have. We made a decision to seek this relationship when we took Step Three.

We took our first action based on that decision in Step Four. We inventoried our faults thoroughly and honestly admitted our shortcomings and defects of character to ourselves and to God. We have begun to discover that resentments, fears, and harmful actions that we have done are the result of our own selfishness, dishonesty, self-centeredness, etc. We are finding that these attitudes are a very real part of us and must be removed if we are to live. We have begun to see the truth that selfishness and self-centeredness are at the core of our problems.

The next required step in the process is to admit these wrongs and their exact nature to another person. This is the Fifth Step of the Program of Recovery.

Having made our personal inventory (Step Four), *what shall we do about it? We have been trying to get a new attitude, a new relationship with our Creator, and to discover the obstacles in our path. We have admitted certain defects: we have ascertained in a rough way what the trouble is; we have put our finger on the weak items in our personal inventory. Now these are about to be cast out. This requires action on our part, which, when completed, will mean that we have admitted to God, to ourselves, and to another human being, the exact nature of our defects. This brings us to the Fifth Step in the program of recovery mentioned in the preceding chapter.*[2]

> **attitude** — state of mind
> **relationship** — connection
> **obstacles** — hindrances
> **defects** — flaws
> **ascertained** — discovered for certain
> **cast out** — removed

Before the things that are blocking us are removed by God, we must humble ourselves in a willing confession of our shortcomings to another person.

This is perhaps difficult — especially discussing our defects with another person. We think we have done well enough in admitting these things to ourselves. There is doubt about that. In actual practice, we usually find a solitary self-appraisal insufficient. Many of us thought it necessary to go much further. We will be more reconciled to discussing ourselves with another person when we see good reasons why we should do so. The best reason first: if we skip

> **solitary** — alone
> **self-appraisal** — examination by ourselves
> **insufficient** — not enough
> **reconciled** — prepared to accept
> **invariably** — without exception
> **persevered** — continued
> **egoism** — self-centeredness

this vital step, we may not overcome drinking. Time after time, newcomers have tried to keep to themselves certain facts about their lives. Trying to avoid this humbling experience, they have turned to easier methods. Almost invariably they got drunk. Having persevered with the rest of the program, they wondered why they fell. We think the reason is that they never completed their housecleaning. They took inventory all right, but hung on to some of the worst items in stock. They only thought that they had lost their egoism and fear; they only thought they had humbled themselves. But they had not learned enough of humility, fearlessness and honesty, in the sense we find it necessary, until they told someone else all their life story.[3]

All of the steps are designed to shrink our tremendous egos, especially Step Five. We have agreed with God and admitted to ourselves our own imperfections, shortcomings, and defects of character, and often feel that is enough. The program of Alcoholics Anonymous and the individuals who wrote it based on their own experience, warn that more is necessary to recover. If we attempt to withhold discussion of our deficiencies by rationalizing and justifying them to ourselves, we will likely remain caught up in our own emotions and will probably drink or use drugs as the result. Our own thinking is not to be trusted. It is better to ask God for the willingness to share the truth of our lives with another person than to live and probably die in our own alcoholism and addictions. Remember that we are relying on God to remove the obsession to use, and easier methods, requiring less humility and honesty, simply don't work.

There is usually fear involved in the taking of this step. We are looking for the truth of who we really are and what is blocking us from the relationship with God that we seek. And we have agreed that we are willing to go to any lengths to do so.

Keep in mind that the Fifth Step is an effort to discuss and share that truth with another person and to discern the "exact nature of our wrongs." Step Five is a discussion between you and your partner, an attempt to ensure that we see that our own selfish, dishonest, self-seeking, fearful, self-reliant, and inconsiderate selves are the root of our problems. These are the exact nature of our wrongs, the things in us that must change for us to live. And we have been living a self-run life for so long that we are likely unable to see that truth unless we are willing to take this humbling step.

When the *Big Book* was written in 1939, there were only a few meetings and the book was being shipped to locations where there were no sponsors or experienced alcoholics with whom to share our Fourth Step. The book had to suggest a variety of persons to do our Fifth Step with, such as religious authorities, doctors, psychologists, various members of our own family, or friends. In 1953, Bill Wilson wrote that our Fifth Step partner might be "someone who is experienced, not necessarily our sponsor."[4] Your sponsor may or may not be the right person to do your Step Five with.

Sponsors are not discussed in the *Big Book* because there were no sponsors when the book was written. Your sponsor should not insist that he or she is the one who must hear your story.

Let him know you are available if he wishes to make a decision and tell his story, but do not insist on it if he prefers to consult someone else.[5]

The important thing is that we go through with this step and are willing to be completely honest with someone about our life. Do not try to anticipate the results or the progression of this step or any other. Understanding will always follow the action, never precede it. The important thing is that we take the action as directed.

We must be entirely honest with somebody if we expect to live long or happily in this world. Rightly and naturally, we think well before we choose the person or persons with whom to take this intimate and confidential step.[6]

intimate — closely personal **confidential** — not to be disclosed

We have no right to save our own skin at another person's expense. Such parts of our story we tell to someone who will understand, yet be unaffected. The rule is that we must be hard on ourselves but always considerate of others.[7]

The person to hear our story should never be someone who will be affected by hearing about the things that we have done. We are to find someone who is not involved in our past life, emotionally or otherwise.

We should prayerfully remain in complete readiness to share our story with the right person when he or she appears. If the person has done a Fifth Step himself, chances are that he will meet our requirements. They will understand the importance and confidentiality of what you are about to do. They will also be pleased to help and should be more likely not to put off the meeting. They have been where you are at and understand the importance of the Fifth Step. This should help to keep you from a delay based on fear or self-rationalization.

The guidelines in the *Big Book* tell us what we are looking for in a Fifth Step partner:

1. That he or she be able to keep whatever we share to him or herself (trustworthy)
2. That he or she fully understand what we are attempting (understanding)
3. That he or she will not try to change our plan (accepting)

It is important that he be able to keep a confidence; that he fully understand and

confidence — trust

approve what we are driving at; that he will not try to change our plan.[8]

When we decide who is to hear our story, we waste no time. We have a written inventory (Step Four) and we are prepared for a long talk. We explain to our partner what we are about to do and why we have to do it. He should realize that we are engaged upon a life-and-death errand. Most people approached in this way will be glad to help; they will be honored by our confidence.[9]

Sharing our shortcomings and defects of character requires an "act of the will" to take the action. If our choice for a Fifth Step partner is someone who has worked the steps and experienced a spiritual awakening, little or no explanation will be necessary.

An experienced partner will also often share some of their own story, his or her own defects of character, to let us know that we are not alone in sharing our past. Alcoholics and addicts running a life based on selfish motives and under the influence of drugs and alcohol in the midst of a spree are capable of anything. Nothing in your inventory will be unique or seen as disgusting by someone who has "been there."

We pocket our pride and go to it, illuminating every twist of character, every dark cranny of the past. Once we have taken this step, withholding nothing, we are delighted. We can look the world in the eye. We can be alone at perfect peace and ease. Our fears fall

pocket — put away	
pride — egoism	
illuminating — revealing	
twist — corner	
cranny — crevice	
delighted — thrilled	
Spirit of the Universe — God	

from us. We begin to feel the nearness of our Creator. We may have had certain spiritual beliefs, but now we begin to have a spiritual experience. The feeling that the drink problem has disappeared will often come strongly. We feel we are on the Broad Highway, walking hand in hand with the Spirit of the Universe.[10]

Notice the need to tell everything to our Fifth Step partner. If we are unwilling or unable to share all of our past, we will not receive the desired and promised results. However, if we have willingly followed the directions and have shared all of our past without holding secrets, some results will be almost immediate.

Shame will begin to leave us and our head will rise. We will begin to experience the freedom of being in a relationship with God. We will begin to know that there not only will be a tomorrow but that it will be better than the past has been. We will begin to truly experience God as we are becoming aware and conscious of Him drawing near.

These are the promises of following the directions and taking the action required to complete Steps Four and Five. Freedom comes from knowing the truth about ourselves, and when this process is completed, we are promised the beginnings of the desired spiritual experience. We will begin to become aware of the reality and the presence of God and His power in our lives and the feeling that the obsession has been removed will often occur. We have faced the things that have been blocking us from God.

We now come to the second time element in specific, precise, and clear-cut directions of recovery. We are to take one hour and review what we have accomplished with God's help and thank Him that we now know Him better.

Returning home we find a place where we can be quiet for an hour, carefully reviewing what we have done. We thank God from the bottom of our heart that we know Him better. Taking this book down from our shelf we turn to the page which contains the twelve steps. Carefully reading the first five proposals we ask if we have omitted anything, for we are building an arch through which we shall walk a free man at last. Is our work solid so far? Are the stones properly in place? Have we skimped on the cement put into the foundation? Have we tried to make mortar without sand?[11]

The outline of the Twelve Steps is found on pages 59 and 60 of the *Big Book*. We are instructed to spend the hour of quiet alone with God and as we review the first five steps on page 59, we are to ask Him to show us if we have been thorough and honest in our working of the steps thus far.

Have we seen the hopelessness and futility of life as we have been living it? Have we honestly seen the truth of that certain death that the obsession of the mind and allergy of our body has condemned us to?

Are we willing to believe that God can remove our obsession of the mind?

Have we truly made the decision to do whatever we must do to let Him have control of our will and our lives?

Have we examined ourselves and discovered that selfishness and self-centeredness are indeed the source of our problems?

Have we been as thorough and honest as we could be and have we shared our shortcomings with another person completely, holding nothing back?

Have we followed the specific, precise, and clear-cut directions to recovery thus far?

If we have deviated or taken short cuts, we will be experiencing something less than what we have been promised. But, if we can prayerfully answer "Yes" to these questions then we have completed the first Five Steps. We are now ready to let God change who and what we have seen that we are without Him.

God Loves Hillbillies

Let me start by saying that I was never a good kid. I acted out constantly and lacked respect for anyone or anything. I discovered later that my childhood had much to do with my anger at the world and lack of "social skills." My step-dad was abusive — both verbally and physically — and I was the victim of sexual molestation by an older cousin. I later found out in going to classes that this was all too common among many alcoholics and drug addicts.

I was sent by my mom to live with my maternal grandmother and she tried her best to raise me, but I pretty much got away with anything I wanted. I was a hillbilly kid from the Ozarks of Missouri and knew that I would never amount to anything just like I had always been told. I hated life and suffered from the pain of it until I found a way to shove that pain deep down inside of myself. I discovered that drugs and alcohol would put pain in a place that I did not have to deal with it. I was young when I found this solution and it worked great. Unfortunately, the alcohol and drug life led me into the jails and drug rehabilitation centers for most of my life from then on. I even completed a one-year-long Drug Court Program, but just like the jails and rehabs, I always returned to the needle and the spoon as soon as I was free of the supervision. I did not know any other way to escape and hide myself from myself. And if there was a God, I knew that he hated hillbillies!

Sixteen or more years of being in trouble or drying out led me to another treatment center. But something different happened this time. They had a man coming in from outside presenting a class on the Twelve Steps of Alcoholics Anonymous.

I thought to myself that alcohol was not my problem, so I had decided not to pay him any attention. Then he drew something he called a "cycle of addiction" up on the board. I was shocked. That was me; that was my entire life from the time I had started to use. I wanted to know how he knew about me. But he talked about his drinking and drug use while trapped in that life and I knew that he knew what he was talking about.

He went on to show me the *Big Book* and talked about the Common Solution Recovery Program. I had to go back home when I finished there to where my mother and grandmother lived. I was facing some very serious charges that I had caught on my last binge and was looking at a probable prison sentence. There was another Church Army in that town and I started going to their classes and I heard the same words about the same book from different people.

I worked those steps and went to court. The judge, who knew me all too well, told me later that he saw something different. He gave me probation when I was looking at a seven year lock-up. I was shocked. I knew that God had given me yet another chance.

That was four years ago and my life is amazing. I have held a job for those years for the first time in my life. I am no longer full of hate and anger and rage. I actually care about other people. The pain has been removed. My teenage daughter now lives with me and my wonderful new wife. That little girl has just as much a new lease on life as I do. My wife and I have bought a house and we own legal vehicles and we now go to church. Life is so much more than I ever thought it could be for someone like me.

I not only have real relationships with other people. I know that I have a real relationship with God, thanks to those steps, but mostly to Him. God has shown me I was wrong. He really does love "hillbillies."

Most people can look back over the years and identify a time and a place at which their lives changed significantly. Whether by accident or design, these are the moments when, because of a readiness within us and collaboration with events occurring around us, we are forced to seriously reappraise ourselves and the conditions under which we live and make certain choices that will affect the rest of our lives.

— Frederick Flack

STEPS SIX AND SEVEN

CHANGE

I became willing to have my new-found Friend take them away, root and branch.[1]

The tendency to relax after Steps Four and Five will be great. We have seen the truth about who we are and what we are apart from God; we have faced our shortcomings and admitted that we are guilty of selfishness and self-centeredness. However, our self-examination in Step Four and our confession of Step Five do not remove the defects of character that we have identified that block us from the personal relationship with God that we are seeking.

Though our decision was a vital and crucial step, it could have little permanent effect unless at once followed by a strenuous effort *to face, **and to be rid of** the things in ourselves which had been blocking us.*[2]

We may feel some relief from the tension of our past, but now we must collect these shortcomings up into a new act of the will and ask God to change us without condition.

We gather the information that we have acquired in Steps Four and Five, the truth about who and what we really are, and in Step Six, prepare to ask God to remove all these objectionable items from us in Step Seven.

If we can answer to our satisfaction, we then look at Step Six. We have emphasized willingness as being indispensable. Are we now ready to let God remove from us all the things which we have ad-

satisfaction — self-approval
emphasized — stressed
indispensable — essential
objectionable — intolerable
cling — hold tightly

mitted are objectionable? Can He now take them all — every one?[3] *If we still cling to something we will not let go, we ask God to help us be willing.*[4]

If we can answer "yes" to the questions at the bottom of page 75, we are ready for Step Six. Step Six is simply asking for willingness to be changed into what God would have us be. We have identified the parts of self that are keeping us from a relationship with God. We have seen that selfishness, along with self-centeredness, dishonesty, fear, self-reliance, and inconsiderate treatment of other people are the root causes of our resentments, fears, harmful acts, and, most importantly, our obsession. We have come to realize that we must be free of these things to survive.

We must change to live. And, being powerless to change ourselves, we must have God's help. We have learned that we cannot wish or will them away in our unaided power. We must be willing to ask God to take all of the things that block us from that relationship with Him. If we are not willing to let go entirely, we do have to be willing to ask God to help us. These flaws are very much a part of our nature. God must supply the necessary power for us to be changed.

We have seen the truth that this selfishness has us in its grip and is more powerful than our will alone. We have wanted to change but were unable to do so in our own power.

We can and must only be willing to believe that God has the power to remove each one of the parts of our nature that block us from Him. There are probably some items that we are unwilling to give up. In fact, we will discover that God will only remove the things that we are willing to surrender to Him. There are usually some parts of our old selfish life that we are not trusting enough or willing enough to let Him take. Being new in our relationship with God, some items, such as relationships, finances, sex, etc. have likely become very important to us. These we must ask God to help us be willing to release if we are unwilling to do so.

Above everything, we alcoholics must be rid of this selfishness. We must, or it kills us! God makes that possible. And there often seems no way of entirely getting rid of self without His aid.[5]

Compare Step Six to being arrested for a crime from our past and appearing in court to find out that we have been charged with "Selfishness and Self-centeredness."

The prosecutor reads the charge and the judge turns to us and asks, "How do you plea?" If we have been thorough and honest in our Fourth Step and have seen that truth magnified in Step Five, we have no choice other than to plead "Guilty." We would then be convicted of the crime and the judge would pass sentence. And the sentence for the real alcoholic is insanity leading to death. We would probably hope to receive a light sentence or even a pardon, but would be powerless to earn it. We need help to escape the penalty for our selfishness.

"I am ready to be offered." It is a transaction of will, not of sentiment. *Tell* God you are ready to be offered, then let the consequences be what they may. There is no strand of complaint now, no matter what God chooses. God puts you through the crisis in private; no one person can help another. Tell God you are ready to be offered, and God will prove Himself to be all you ever dreamed He would be.[6]

When ready, we say something like this: "My Creator, I am now willing that you should have all of me, good and bad. I pray that you now remove from me every single defect of character which stands in the way of my useful- **bidding — will** *ness to you and my fellows. Grant me strength, as I go out to do your bidding. Amen."*[7]

Step Seven is a simple but powerful prayer asking God to remove from us the character defects that we have identified as the root cause of our problems. In Step Three we offered as much of ourselves as we knew to as much of God as we could understand. Now, after seeing the truth of what is blocking us from Him in Steps Four and Five, we have become aware of the need to gather ourselves into a new surrender to the God that we have come to know better and allow Him to change the parts of self that hinder us from doing His will.

We ask Him to take all of us. Not only the bad things that we know interfere with our relationship with Him, but also the things that we perceive as good in ourselves. In other words, we offer all of ourselves, assets and liabilities alike.

We now pray to Him to remove everything that stands in our way of knowing Him better and doing His will in our lives. Every single thing that could stop us from working for Him and helping others.

Finally, we ask Him for the strength to carry out His will. And, if we have been honest and have followed directions, God will always say "yes" to a prayer that aligns with His will.

In Step Three we made a decision to seek to turn over our wills and our lives to the care of God as we understood Him. Steps Four through Seven are the action steps that we take to allow God to make that decision become a reality in our lives.

Note that the prayer of Step Seven ends with "Amen," where Step Three does not. When we say "Amen" we are praying "So be it" or affirming our agreement with what we have just prayed. God's will and our will are in line at this moment.

The prayer of Step Three on page 63 of the *Big Book* was a plea to God to help us take the actions that followed, and when I have completed Step Seven, my prayer has been answered and likely the obsession has been removed whether or not I am aware of it.

We have now completed Step Seven.[8]

Testimony

Waiting for the Other Shoe to Drop

Six years ago, after a lifetime of trying to control everyone and everything around me, there came the day when my probation officer did an intervention of sorts. She was an alcoholic herself and knew of a place called Church Army where I got my first real taste of recovery and the Twelve Steps. However, I was not yet ready to stop my drinking and drug use. I was asked to leave.

My return to the streets resulted in more pain and worse suffering than I had ever experienced. I had finally had enough of that life and was willing to do whatever it took to stay sober. I returned to that program. I was determined to use the tools that they were offering me this time. I moved into a sober-living house, got a good job, and everything seemed to be going well as I was attending classes and meetings and not drinking or using drugs.

One day my sponsor told me that there was no need to meet with him anymore. Not because I was doing so well but because it was obvious to him that I was not interested in long-term recovery. He was talking about working the "steps" as they were being presented to me in the Common Solution Recovery Classes.

I wanted what he had with everything that was in me, but had missed the truth that I must be willing to put the work and time into the program and trust in God and not myself to achieve just that.

After careful consideration and the writing required in Step Four and sharing all my "little secrets" in Step Five, followed by the changes brought about in Steps Six and Seven, I felt a cleansing a lot like I had been baptized.

Well, that was almost five years ago and I am doing things in my life which I never thought were possible. I have made many of my amends, including those to my family. We have slowly pieced things back together; I have walked my daughter down the aisle on her wedding day and I am helping my son go to college.

My abused wife (who I blamed all my problems on) and I have been reunited. We have been able to purchase our own home. I have my mom and dad and the rest of my family back in my life and more real friends than I ever thought could be.

I have learned that God is good, that God is great, and from working those simple steps I have learned to put everything in His hands. Above all, I have learned that there is a power greater than myself, a loving God that could and did restore me to sanity. I have come to understand that the relationship with my Lord and Savior, Jesus Christ, must come first above anything or anyone else. And to do that, all I have to do is live my life through the working of the same steps that I was given those years ago.

I lived my former life in fear of when the next problem would catch up to me. Today, through this program, I live my life without that fear of "waiting for the other shoe to drop."

I am truly blessed. I thank God that he put that man in my path to speak the truth to me in love and for the Twelve Steps that gave me a way out of that life as I was living it!

Life is relationship; the rest is just details.
— Gary Smalley

STEPS EIGHT AND NINE

AMENDS

*We made a list of people I had hurt or toward whom
I felt resentment. I expressed my entire willingness to
approach these individuals, admitting my wrong. Never
was I to be critical of them. I was to right all such matters
to the utmost of my ability.*[1]

We have experienced willingness as being the key to our spiritual growth. We had to have willingness to face the truth of our problem, a willingness to believe and to examine ourselves, a willingness to share our shortcomings and defects of character with another person and, finally, a willingness to be changed. Now that we have experienced God's Power affecting a change in our thinking, we must have more willingness to take the action to repair the damage done to others in our past by our former lifestyle.

Before we continue into Steps Eight and Nine, we should again be aware of the instructions for the rest of the program. Steps Ten, Eleven, and Twelve contain the instructions for how we should live as soon as we have experienced the results of Step Seven.

Step Nine is a step that we will probably be working for some time. The problem is that if we wait to begin to work Steps Ten, Eleven, and Twelve until after we have completed making all of our amends, we will be allowing new resentments, fears, and damaging actions to pour back into our lives.

There are specific time elements in the directions for recovery as contained in the *Big Book of Alcoholics Anonymous*. Remember, the first was between Steps Three and Four. We were to begin work on our written inventory as soon as we had made a decision to go through with the program.

The instruction was on page 64, paragraph 1. We were told *"Though our decision was a vital and crucial step, it could have little permanent effect unless **at once** followed by a strenuous effort to face, and to be rid of, the things which had been blocking us."*

The next instruction given regarding time was on Page 75, paragraph 4, after we had shared the exact nature of our wrongs with our Fifth Step partner. *"Returning home we find a place where we can be quiet for **an hour**, carefully reviewing what we have done."*

Turn to page 84, third paragraph, to see our third specific "when" direction. *"This thought brings us to Step Ten, which suggests we continue to take personal inventory and continue to set right any new mistakes **as we go along**. We vigorously commenced this way of living **as we cleaned up the past**."*

We cannot wait until all of our amends in Step Nine are completed before we begin working Step Ten. The danger in doing so is apparent. Selfishness and self-centeredness can and will creep back into our lives if we are not growing in our relationship with God as we live our lives each day. If we delay taking the steps that are required to grow spiritually in our daily lives until all of our amends are complete, undoubtedly resentment and fear based on our selfish nature will return and inevitably be followed by the obsession to drink or use drugs.

We must begin taking the actions of Steps Ten, Eleven, and Twelve as we work Step Nine. Step Eight is a once-done step, but Step Nine will likely be an ongoing effort to repair the damage that our self-directed life has caused for some time.

*Now we need more action, without which we find that "Faith without works is dead." Let's look at **Steps Eight and Nine**. We have a list of persons we harmed and to whom we are willing to make amends. We made it when we took inventory. We subjected ourselves to a drastic self-apprais-al. Now we go out to our fellows and repair the damage done in the past. We attempt to sweep away the debris which has accumulated out of our effort to live on self-will and run the show ourselves. If we haven't the will to do this, we ask until it comes. Remember, it was agreed at the beginning that **we would go to any lengths for victory over alcohol.**[2]*

> **commenced** — began
> **drastic** — far-reaching
> **self-appraisal** — assessment of our self
> **debris** — wreckage
> **accumulated** — piled up

Willingness followed by action is the key to recovery in the program of Alcoholics Anonymous.

The *Big Book* tells us that we have compiled a list of persons we have harmed. This list is our written Fourth Step that contains all the people that we have harmed with our selfish judgments, beliefs, and actions. Column One of our resentment sheet, our fear inventory, and our sex conduct summary will have many individuals listed.

These are the persons that we must be willing to go to and make our amends. Step Nine requires a willingness to face these people on our Fourth Step and attempt to set right our wrongs. This willingness is what we pray for in Step Eight. If we are not willing, we continue to ask God for it until it comes.

Step Eight is also a time to look at our inventory list and be sure that no one would be harmed if they read it. The directions do not tell us to make a new list, but experience has shown us that some Fourth Step paperwork should be destroyed after we have transferred the list to a separate sheet that would not harm others if it was accidently read.

It has become a popular practice to destroy our Fourth Step papers when Step Five is completed. *WARNING: Do not dispose of your Step Four until you have transferred the necessary information to your amends list.*

The *Big Book* masterfully covers the required amends process necessary to set past relationships with others straight. We will never come fully clean with our past until we fully accept responsibility for it. The amends process is an ongoing effort to straighten up our past lives by accepting accountability for our wrongs and taking the necessary action to repair our past. If we are unwilling to go through with the amends process, we ask God for the required willingness. If we won't ask Him for help then we are working some program other than the program of *Alcoholics Anonymous*.

The key to Step Nine is the willingness that is found in Step Eight. Once we have asked for that willingness to repair our past wrongs, we will find that the fear of taking the action will be overcome.

Remember, we have discovered a process to rise above our fear when we did our Fourth Step.[3] We identify it and we ask God to take it from us and direct our attention to what He would have us be. The fear of making the amends will abate as we pray for the willingness to take the required action.

Mark Twain once said, "Courage is mastery of fear — not absence of fear."

There are many forms and types of amends that we will be required to make. Though these amends will take numerous forms, we will discover that the experience of the first alcoholics shared in detail on page 76 through page 84 can serve as a fundamental and reliable guide in the process.

As we study these pages, we will see how the *Big Book* covers in a general way each amend that we will encounter in cleaning up our past.

It offers advice and guidance in most, if not all, the different situations that may arise during the process of making our amends. Amends covered include problems with our past enemies, with financial problems, with the courts, and with other legal problems. The *Big Book* also addresses amends in the area of extramarital sex, jealousy, spouses, and other immediate family members, and even offers advice in the area of amends that we cannot make directly, such as persons who have died or cannot be seen face-to-face.

These areas are covered in detail and suggestions can be found throughout the pages of the *Big Book* that address the amends process:

*The question of how to approach the **man we hated** will arise.*[4]

This is the person on our list of resentments that we probably feel has done us much more harm than we have done him or her. We will probably be hesitant to approach them. Remember that we have asked God to help us to show them the same tolerance, pity, and patience that we would cheerfully grant a sick friend. We will possess a new attitude of forgiveness and kindness. We should explain what we are doing there, confessing our former ill feeling and sticking to our own faults.

The result of our visit is in God's hands, regardless of whether old feuds are repaired or he throws us out of his house. We have made the effort; we have done our part.

*We do not dodge our **creditors**. We must lose our fear of creditors no matter how far we have to go, for we are liable to drink if we are afraid to face them.*[5]

We have likely been avoiding those people to whom we owe money. Now we have the courage to contact them and work out a payment plan based on the truth about our past problems and our effort to live a different life. We are also to be honest with them about our current financial situation. Again, we are relying on God for the courage to face the people to whom we owe financial amends. Many alcoholics have been surprised to find that God has provided the needed finances to make payments to our creditors as we become willing to take this step. Regardless, we must face our fear of creditors or risk using again.

*Perhaps we have committed a **criminal offense**. . . .*[6]

These amends could come from any of our three lists. Criminal offenses can take many forms in the life of an alcoholic and addict and are considered common. They will include old warrants, unpaid child support, outstanding tickets and fines, and stealing from our employer or relatives. Many alcoholics and addicts have some sort of criminal activity in their past. We must not avoid our responsibility in facing up to them. The *Big Book* is very clear on how, when, and even if we should do so.

*Usually, however, **other people** are involved.*[7]

Amends that involve other persons, such as criminal offenses, marital infidelity, employers, etc. should never be made without clear permission from the persons that will be affected if we go through with our plan. Many of these amends cannot be made because the other person is unwilling to allow us to cause damage to them. We must remain willing to make these amends but we cannot make them directly without the needed consent.

*The chances are we have **domestic** troubles.*[8]

The personal life of an alcoholic/addict is usually in turmoil when we begin the recovery process. Drinking and drugs and selfishness have resulted in extramarital affairs in many of our lives. The *Big Book* lays down no specific rules in this area of our amends because other people are always involved and many unsuspecting persons can be harmed with these amends. It is very important that we stay close to the basic principles in this area and that we trust God to guide us through these areas.

. . . there is plenty we should do at **home.**[9]

The alcoholic's home is rarely unaffected by our former life. Children, spouses, and parents may be frightened or disgusted. Relationships with our family will often take time to repair. Staying sober will help but will never be enough. The *Big Book* suggests that we sit down with our family and honestly look at the past and our own mistakes while being careful not to talk about theirs. The demonstration of our newly acquired spiritual principles will convince them and may, in time, lead them to follow us in our spiritual journey.

There may be some **wrongs we can never fully right.** *Some* **people cannot be seen.**[10]

There will likely be some on our amends list that cannot be made directly to our satisfaction. Some people will have died or they cannot be seen for many other reasons. To make the amends would possibly damage them or others. Many of the people that we have harmed with our sexual conduct will fall into this category. We do not know their names, they cannot be located, or possibly the wounds are still too fresh. The key is the willingness to see them and make the amends if we could. We trust God in these matters.

We cannot make direct amends to some people at times. The *Big Book* tells us that we can send them a letter. Many will use this sentence out of context as an excuse to write letters instead of making direct amends. The problem with making amends through the mail is that we have no idea where we stand with the person; we don't know if they received the letter or not. We don't know if they actually read the letter or tore it up without reading it when they received it. Oldtimers often say, "If you harmed them with a letter, then you can make the amends with a letter."

Some amends cannot be made right now; some can never be made. The key is that we must be willing to trust God to place that person in our lives wherever the time is right. Some amends will simply have to remain unmade and lived with by God's grace.

Though there are no rules for making amends, the *Big Book* offers some guidelines that can and should be applied to every amend that we make and to the overall process itself.

At the moment we are trying to put our lives in order. But this is not an end in itself. Our real purpose is to fit ourselves to be of maximum service to God and the people about us.[11]

We came to work the steps because our lives had become unmanageable. Our lives were in disarray and the process of working the steps allowed God to create order out of that chaos. But this must not be our only motive. If it is, we are remaining selfish.

In the Seventh Step, we asked God to remove from us every single defect of character that stands in the way of our usefulness to Him and our fellows.[12] The amends process is the action required to do just that. It is clear that we can never be in the relationship with God that we so desire and desperately need until we are in right relationship with people. We never can come fully clean with our life until we take full responsibility for how we have lived it.[13]

But our man is sure to be impressed with a sincere desire to set right the wrong. He is going to be more interested in a demonstration of good will than in our talk of spiritual discoveries.[14]

The definition of *amend* is to attempt to set right the wrong, not just to make an apology. How many times have we made apologies and turned right around and repeated the offenses that caused us to say "I'm sorry" in the first place? Many of us have talked about changing many times in the past to the people that we owe the amends. We must now show them with our actions that something is truly different in our lives.

Under no condition do we criticize such a person or argue.[15]

We must stop passing judgment on others. If we go to our man in a helpful and forgiving spirit, not discussing his faults but our own and we meet him in a calm and honest way, we will likely be more than satisfied with the results. We prayed in Step Eight for the willingness to make these amends and God will provide the power for us to carry them through.

Reminding ourselves that we have decided to go to any lengths to find a spiritual experience, we ask that we be given strength and direction to do the right thing, no matter what the personal consequences might be.[16]

The mental conclusions of Steps One and Two, knowing the depth and weight of our problem and a willingness to believe that a Power greater than ourselves would be needed to recover, were required to get us to the decision point of taking action. On the weight of that decision, we took the action required to seek the recovery that the first recovered alcoholics who wrote the *Big Book* had and we were "willing to go to any lengths to get it."[17]

When we prayed for the willingness to take the action required to make amends, we were reminded that "we would go to any lengths for victory over alcohol."[18]

Regardless of the possible repercussions that we face when making amends, we must not turn away. We might be humiliated, we may face the loss of a job or imprisonment, but we must be willing to do so. We must take this difficult step or remain blocked off from God. We may never experience a spiritual awakening which we have said we were willing to go to any lengths to get. And without spiritual growth, the obsession will return and we will drink or use and be faced with an early death.

We must not shrink at anything.[19]

The Ninth Step as written on page 59 of the *Big Book* says that we made direct amends to such people wherever possible, except when to do so would injure them or others.

Note that the step says ". . . wherever possible" not "whenever." Wherever speaks to both time and place. God makes both of these possible and we can place our confidence in Him to provide them. If we are trying to decide when to make our amends, we are likely to never find just the right time or place if left to our own choices. Once again, willingness is the key.

> WARNING: The book never tells us that we are to be careful of not injuring ourselves because we are an "other." This is a misleading lie to selfishly rationalize our way out of the process that often circulates in recovery groups and is a dangerous excuse to avoid making amends. We are not an "other." We must become willing to go to any lengths for our sobriety regardless of the consequences to ourselves.

Do not, however, let the fear of the difficult, threatening amend keep you from making it, with the exception being that there may be other persons involved who will be affected by them.

Therefore, we are not to be the hasty and foolish martyr who would needlessly sacrifice others to save himself from the alcoholic pit.[20]

The *Big Book* gives us a great example of this principle on page 79 and 80. A man owed alimony to an ex-wife and she had a warrant issued for his arrest. He was working the program, had gotten a job, and was doing well. He was willing to turn himself in to the authorities if it became necessary.

However, the man had remarried and had a new family to think about, as well as his employer. It was suggested that he take the action to send his first wife some money in a letter and make arrangements for payment of what was owed. He did and the situation was resolved.

Before taking drastic action which might implicate other people we secure their consent.[21]

The *Big Book* tells us that we cannot save ourselves if we must continue hurting others while doing so. That is self-centered and self-serving and it should be obvious to us by now that selfishness will never fit God's plan. We should talk it over with those who might be affected, and we should discuss the amends with our sponsor and others whose experience we trust. If we have asked God for direction and the step is still called for, we must be willing to make the amend.

The spiritual life is not a theory. We have to live it.[22]

Our actions in making amends will result in much more change than our words. Remember, our spouses, children, and other relatives, as well as our friends, co-workers, and employers have probably heard the words before. They have every right to be skeptical. We would be too, if the roles were reversed. Our actions will speak louder than our words, and if we have worked the steps and are willing to be led by God, then our dealings with them will be filled with kindness and will demonstrate the change that all of them have been waiting and praying for all along.

The Ninth Step Promises are found on pages 83 and 84 of the *Big Book*. They are often read in meetings and called the Promises. Many newcomers are confused by this and are usually afraid to ask what they mean. They are promised only to those who are working the spiritual principles that are the Program of Alcoholics Anonymous, specifically as a result of making the called-for amends.

The Promises of the Ninth Step will come to us during the amends process. Although read at many meetings and alcoholic and addict treatment facilities, it should be made clear that these Promises are part of a progression. The alcoholic must make the mental conclusions of Steps One and Two, followed by the decision to turn our thinking and our actions over to God in Step Three. We fulfill this decision by following the directions of Steps Four, Five, Six, and Seven to examine ourselves, admit our wrongs, and willingly allow God to remove the things that are responsible for keeping us from being the person that He intended us to be. This change of heart and mind is followed with the willingness to be in right relationship with others and to set right the wrongs of our past.

The Promises of Step Nine come only as the result of working all the steps in order following the specific, precise, and clear-cut directions as they are given to us in the *Big Book*.

NINTH STEP PROMISES[23]

1. If we are painstaking about this phase of our development, we will be amazed before we are halfway through.

2. We are going to know a new freedom and a new happiness.

3. We will not regret the past nor wish to shut the door on it.

4. We will comprehend the word serenity and we will know peace.

painstaking — conscientious, thorough
phase — period
know — experience
regret — feel sorry for ourselves
comprehend — understand
serenity — calmness
scale — measuring stick
benefit — help

5. *No matter how far down the scale we have gone, we will see how our experience can benefit others.*

6. *That feeling of uselessness and self-pity will disappear.*

7. *We will lose interest in selfish things and gain interest in our fellows.*

fellows — others
self-seeking — selfish actions based on personal desires
outlook — point of view
economic — financial
insecurity — anxiety
intuitively – instinctively
baffle — confuse
realize — become aware of

8. *Self-seeking will slip away.*

9. *Our whole attitude and outlook on life will change.*

10. *Fear of people and of economic insecurity will leave us.*

11. *We will intuitively know how to handle situations which used to baffle us.*

12. *We will suddenly realize that God is doing for us what we could not do for ourselves.*

The promises of intentionally taking the action to repair the damage caused by our selfish nature in our past will always come true *if we make the amends*. Rapid spiritual growth will likely happen during this process. Willingness followed by action is the key to Steps Eight and Nine. Neither can be omitted.

Bill Wilson wrote that Step Nine is the beginning of the end of isolation from our fellows and from God.[24]

This Can't Be Real. They Can't Be Real

A little over three years ago I was lost and my life had gone spinning out of control. I had rejected everything and everyone that loved me, including my three children. I was a hopeless crack addict and wanted to die. But instead of death, I went to jail after jail and faced situations on a daily basis that would terrify a sane and normal person. All I cared about was my next fix and where would I get it. When I would get high, I was willing to do anything to get higher.

After countless attempts at treatment for my addiction, my daughter convinced me to give it one last chance. I had been in that last treatment center for a week when a counselor asked me to visit a place called Church Army. The name sounded very strange and I was reluctant to go even for a day. But realizing that I had nothing to lose, I went on the trip with some others from the center.

When we got there we were shown around and then taken into a classroom and shown something that they called the "cycle of addiction." I saw my life placed right in front of me up on a chalkboard. They showed me why I couldn't stop going back to the drugs; why I couldn't stop using.

I thought to myself, *This can't be real. They can't be real. How do they know me so well? What is this all about?* I was excited beyond words. I went back and finished my 28 days and returned to that place and those people. That program had me and I wanted more. I wanted what everyone else seemed to have. That was joy and peace and real friendships.

There I sat through the Common Solution Recovery classes and worked the Twelve Steps like they told me to — admit that I am truly powerless, be willing to believe that there was a God who wanted to help me, and make a decision to seek the solution that was offered. I went on to work the Fourth and Fifth Steps and discover how truly selfish and separated from God I had been my whole life. I was ready to have God change me. I simply asked Him to do just that and to give me the courage to repair the damage my life had caused so many people as best I could. The best part was that I got to help the next person that came in those doors and share with them what had been given to me.

I could never put it all into words the amazing peace that I have found as the result of working these steps. My life has been transformed and so have the lives of those who love me and many, many others. I have gotten married, have survived cancer, and helped many, many people find recovery in the few years since I have recovered.

I will never stop being grateful for the gift that was given to me in the Twelve Steps and for the instructions on how to work them. I know that without them, I would be dead now or worse, still living in that cycle of addiction.

I love my life today, I love people and most of all, I love the God who loves me.

There is a difference between knowing
the path and walking the path.
— Morpheus, in the film *The Matrix*

Prayer may not change things for you,
but it for sure changes you for things.
— Samuel M. Shoemaker

STEPS TEN AND ELEVEN

SELF-EXAMINATION, PRAYER, AND MEDITATION

*I was to test my thinking by the new God-
consciousness within. Common sense would thus
become uncommon sense. I was to sit quietly when in
doubt, asking only for direction and strength to meet
my problems as He would have me.*[1]

We have done much and been given much in the first steps
of this program. Steps Ten and Eleven will serve as ongoing
tools for spiritual growth when they are practiced as a way of
life. They are not independent of one another; in fact, they are
intertwined and closely knit and will not be effective if practiced one without the other.

Bill Wilson writes of this in the Twelve and Twelve:

*There is a direct linkage among self-examination, meditation, and
prayer. Taken separately, these practices can bring much relief and*

benefit. But when they are logically related and interwoven, the result is an unshakable foundation for life.[2]

We have learned in working the steps that it is vital to grow in relationship with God or our sobriety will be soon lost.

We have inventoried the defects of character that interfere with and block us off from that desired relationship. Steps Ten and Eleven will assure us that we will be able to continue to seek to discover and to do the will of God, and in doing so will continue in our recovery, free of the obsession to use drugs and alcohol.

Step Ten, continuing to watch for the shortcomings that block us off from that relationship with God, is required to make our prayer life effective, and prayer and meditation (Step Eleven) is necessary for us to have the power and desire to seek to identify the flaws in our make-up.

One without the other is unproductive for the real alcoholic or real addict and will soon lead to a return to our old self-run life. If we attempt to self-police our own lives we will fail; we must always remember that we are powerless to do so.

We have been graced with a new relationship with God through the working of the steps and we now must build and grow upon that foundation. We must continue in this new way of life.

Step Ten – *Continued to take personal inventory and when we were wrong promptly admitted it.*[3]

*This thought brings us to Step Ten, which suggests we **continue** to take personal inventory and **continue** to set right any new mistakes as we go along. We vigorously commenced this way of living as we cleaned up the past. We have entered the world of the Spirit. Our next function is to grow in understanding and effectiveness. This is not an overnight matter. It should*

---

vigorously — with much effort
commenced — began
effectiveness — usefulness

continue *for a lifetime.* **Continue** *to watch for selfishness, dishonesty, resentment and fear. When these*

resolutely — purposefully
code — policy

crop up, we ask God at once to remove them. We discuss them with someone immediately and make amends quickly if we harmed anyone. Then we resolutely turn our thoughts to someone we can help. Love and tolerance of others is our code.[4]

This thought . . . the thought is that God keeps His promises regardless of how we feel at this time in our working of the steps. If we have been as thorough and as honest as we are capable of in working the process, the truth is that God is now doing for us what we could never do for ourselves. Our part is to be willing to follow the working directions.

Continue, continue, continue. . . . We cannot continue to do something that we have never started. Step Ten cannot be put into practice without having experienced the results of Steps Four through Nine.

. . . as we cleaned up the past. We are to begin working Steps Ten through Twelve as we begin our amends process. Step Nine will likely be a long process which may never be completed. We are instructed to begin to practice maintenance of our spiritual condition as soon as we have begun to make our amends. This is the third time element in the precise directions given to us in the *Big Book*.

. . . the world of the Spirit. Up until now, we have been living in the world of our own selfishness and self-centeredness. The world of God's Spirit is where an alcoholic or addict must live to survive. The *Big Book* in two places calls this the fourth dimension of existence.[5] The fourth dimension cannot be described or explained. It must be experienced.

. . . grow in understanding and effectiveness. We must be growing spiritually or we are always in danger of losing what we have obtained. As we continue working the Steps of Alcoholics Anonymous, we will continue to grow in our

understanding of God and His Power and this growth will increase our usefulness to Him and to the people around us.

. . . continue for our lifetime. Spiritual growth must continue everyday in the practice of these principles "one day at a time." The final three steps of Alcoholics Anonymous are meant to be practiced as a way of life. They are never to be considered as a once-done event or "sometimes" way of living to be used only when we feel the need.

Continue to watch. . . . We are to continue to be alert for the things in us that interfere with our new relationship with God. We learned to do this when working **Step Four**. Selfishness, dishonesty, resentment, and fear are those manifestations of self that indicate that we are trying to take back control of our own lives from God.

When these crop up. . . . We will never be 100 percent spiritually fit in this lifetime. We will sometimes, possibly often, slip back into self-reliance and self-centeredness. When something difficult or troublesome occurs in our life, we will possibly react to the event with selfishness, dishonesty, resentment, or fear. We are instructed to view these responses as symptoms of our own spiritual sickness and take them to God just as we would go to the doctor with a physical problem.

. . . we ask God at once to remove them. We are learning to rely on God to do for us what we can't do for ourselves, and just as we did in **Steps Six and Seven**, we are willing to be changed and we ask God to change us. We do this as soon as we identify the problem that is in us. If we delay, we remain in our selfishness and remain vulnerable to the obsession to use returning.

We discuss them with someone immediately. Just as we did in **Step Five**, we are willing to discuss our wrongs and the action that may be called for to set matters straight in the situation with another person that we trust. We may need the scrutiny of someone who is independent of and unaffected by the situation to help us see the truth of the matter.

. . . and make amends quickly if we have harmed anyone. **Steps Eight and Nine.** A willingness to set right a wrong we may have done to another person is vital to our spiritual growth. If we are unwilling to attempt to set right our part in the conflict, we are likely to harbor resentments.

Step Ten is to be continually practiced as the day goes on. It is often referred to as our "walking around step." Step Ten is *not* something we do once a day or at night before we go to bed. Our selfishness can build up to a point of giving power to the obsession to use to return and we will have to drink or use, possibly before the day is over.

Love and tolerance of others is our code. When the selfishness that has blocked us from a relationship with God is removed, we will find as we practice these steps, that we are more patient and loving towards people. This is a sure sign that God is working in us and through us to care about others and how we may serve them. Just the opposite, hate and intolerance are sure indicators of selfishness and self-centeredness. They are the twin markers of our old self trying to once again be in control.

The *Big Book* Promises of Step Ten are given to anyone who has had a spiritual awakening as the result of taking the action required to recover. They are not promised to those who are working another program or attempting some other method of recovery. They are what most of us were seeking when we began working the steps.

1. *And we have ceased fighting anything or anyone — even alcohol.*[6]

ceased — stopped

   We have finally truly admitted that we are powerless over alcohol and other addictive substances; we have lost every time we fought against our addictions on our own power. We have been given the gift of complete defeat. As a result, we stop struggling and battling with our addictions and allow God to take control.

2. *For by this time sanity will have returned.*[7] In Step Two, we only had to be willing to believe that God could restore us to sanity in the area of the first drink. The *Big Book* promises us that through the working of the steps, we will now be able to see the truth about the first drink. We will be restored to sanity when the obsession to drink has been removed. This is what it means to be a recovered alcoholic.

3. *We will seldom be interested in liquor.*[8] Our thoughts are no longer being controlled by the insane thinking that we can safely drink alcohol or use drugs.

4. *If tempted, we recoil as from a hot flame.*[9] If the thought does cross our

recoil — react

   minds that we can safely drink or use, the program of the *Big Book* promises that we will react as we would react to the threat of being burned by fire.

5. *We react sanely and normally, and we will find that this has happened automatically.*[10] This sane and normal reaction happens without any exertion on our part other than willingness to attempt to seek and to stay in right relationship with God. God is the power, not ourselves. He has removed the obsession to use from our minds, usually without our even being aware of it.

6. *We will see that our new attitude toward liquor has been given us without any thought or effort on our part. It just comes! That is the miracle of it.*[11] God has given us a new mindset toward alcohol and drug use, and when the obsession is removed, it is done entirely by God's power and none of our own. To the real alcoholic or

addict who has been consumed by the passion to use and sometimes struggled for many years to overcome the desire only to give in to it time and time again, this experience is nothing short of miraculous.

7. *We are not fighting it, neither are we avoiding temptation.*[12] We have admitted that we are powerless and know

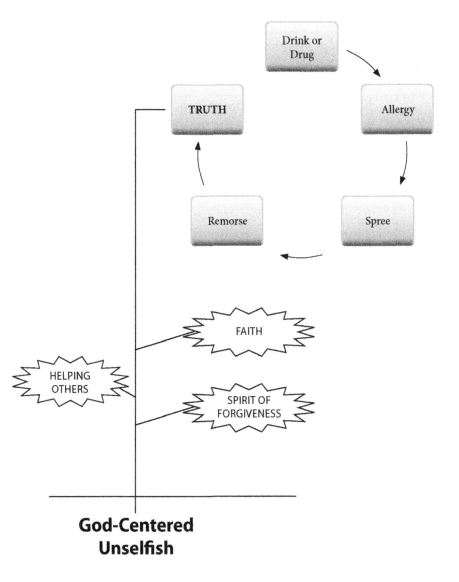

**God-Centered
Unselfish**

from past experience that we can do nothing in our unaided human strength to win the fight to stay sober, including avoidance of places and persons that might cause us problems. We no longer need to combat the problem by hiding from it. If I am recovered, the insane thought that always preceded the using has been replaced and I am free to go anywhere I need to so long as I am spiritually fit.[13]

8. *We feel as though we had been placed in a position of neutrality — safe and protected.*[14] We are now made to feel secure by God as the result of working the Steps of Alcoholics Anonymous as instructed. We should experience a sense of detachment for the debate of legalization of drugs or the battle between drinkers and non-drinkers over the benefits or damage caused by social drinking.

9. *We have not even sworn off. Instead the problem has been removed. It does not exist for us.*[15] Swearing off is a human resource that we have found will not work in the life of drinkers and drug users of our type. God must have removed our obsession to drink and use — no human power could have. The *Big Book* promises that as the result of working the steps, God has reached into my mind and expelled the obsession to drink and replaced it with truth in the area of the first drink. The problem is gone from my life; it has disappeared.

10. *We are neither cocky nor are we afraid.* The recovered alcoholic should have no confidence in himself nor should he constantly remain fearful of returning to alcohol and drugs for a solution to his problems. God has done for him what he could not do for himself!

That is our experience. That is how we react so long as we keep in fit spiritual condition.[16]

The *Big Book* is a book of experience, not of theories or ideas. The first recovered alcoholics wrote the *Big Book* to share with others the way in which they found a way out of the hopeless pit of alcoholism and addiction. The Promises of Step Ten are based on the results that they received from working all of the steps and tell us that we will also continue to receive them as long as we grow in our relationship with God.

It is easy to let up on the spiritual program of action and rest on our laurels. We are headed for trouble if we do, for alcohol is a subtle foe. We are not cured of alcoholism. What we really have is a daily reprieve contingent upon the maintenance of our spiritual condition. Every day is a day when we must carry the vision of God's will into all of our activities.

laurels — achievements
subtle — clever
foe — enemy
cured — healed
reprieve — relief
contingent — conditional
maintenance — upkeep
activities — actions
constantly — all the time
exercise — implement

"How can I best serve Thee —Thy will (not mine) be done." These thoughts must go with us constantly. We can exercise our will power along this line all we wish. It is the proper use of the will.[17]

The success that we have experienced in our recovery is only by the grace of God and is never of our own making. The *Big Book* warns us that it is easy to be trapped into believing that we have done something to achieve or to earn our sobriety. Well-meaning friends and relatives, in and out of the rooms of AA, will praise us for what we have done. Remember, we are to always give God the credit for our sobriety. Any other type of thinking could easily result in disaster.

Recovered does not mean cured. We must continue to grow in our relationship with God and continue to maintain that relationship to be guided by Him. We will always be alcoholics and addicts, but we can become and remain recovered alcoholics and addicts. But we must never assume that we can safely drink or use again under any circumstances. We have simply been given the freedom to see this fundamental truth, and so by definition, we have been restored to mental health in the area of our alcohol and drug use.

Our willpower, under the guidance of a sane, God-directed mind can now be used correctly. Man's thinking is only truly his own when it is under God's guidance. When man's will and God's will align, it is a sure recipe for peace in our lives.

Much has been said about receiving strength, inspiration and direction from Him who has all knowledge and power. If we have carefully followed directions, we have begun to sense the flow of His Spirit into us. To

> **extent** — degree
> **develop** — grow
> **vital** — necessary to live

some extent we have become God-conscious. We have begun to develop this vital sixth sense. But we must go further and that means more action.[18]

As we practice the spiritual principles as directed in the program contained in the text of the *Big Book of Alcoholics Anonymous,* we will begin to become aware of God's presence in our thinking and our actions. In the past we have always had to rely on our senses of touch, taste, hearing, sight, and smell in our decision-making process. Now the *Big Book* promises us that we will begin to develop a sixth sense. This sixth sense that we cannot see, touch, taste, feel, or hear is the sense of faith. We will begin to trust that God is doing for us what we could never have done for ourselves, regardless of how situations may appear to us at a given moment.

We have become convinced that not only is there a God, but He cares for us in a way that we could never before imagine. But more is required if we are to continue to grow in this relationship and in our awareness of God. More action is needed.

Step Eleven — *Sought through prayer and meditation to improve our conscious contact with God as we understood Him, praying only for the knowledge of His will for us and the power to carry that out.* [19]

Bill Wilson was less than three years sober when he wrote down the information to work Step Eleven. Bill's background shows us that he obviously was not a theological giant or great religious leader, but he knew that to grow in relationship with God that regular prayer and meditation would be required. Amazingly enough, these pages for a suggested prayer life have given many thousands of people a way to communicate with God.

Many of us feel in early sobriety that we cannot work this program because we don't know how to pray. When I confronted my sponsor with this dilemma, he said, "Don't worry about it. Work the steps as they are laid out for you and the Holy Spirit of God will enter your life and teach you how to pray."

Step Eleven is broken down to three distinct areas of each day. The instructions give us suggestions on prayer and meditation before going to sleep at night, when I wake up in the morning, and as I go through the activities of each day.

When we retire at night*, we constructively review our day. Were we selfish, dishonest, or afraid? Do we owe an apology? Have we kept something to ourselves which should be discussed with another person at once? Were we kind and loving toward all? What could we have done better? Were we thinking of ourselves most of the time? Or were we thinking of what we could do for others, of what we could pack into the stream of life? But we must be careful not to drift into worry, remorse, or morbid reflection, for that would diminish our usefulness*

constructively — usefully	
review — examine	
apology — amend	
stream — flow	
drift — wander	
depressing — reflection	
inquire — ask	

to others. After making our review we ask God's forgiveness and inquire what corrective measures should be taken.[20]

The purpose of the nighttime review is to go back over our day and see if we failed to address any issues resulting from our selfishness and self-centeredness as we applied Step Ten in our daily walk. It is not meant to replace the actions of Step Ten. We repeat the process of examining ourselves for short-comings in our life for that day. We answer the question of what selfish act we had neglected to address or even recognize at the time that it took place. The *Big Book* warns us not to be remorseful when we see our part in these occurrences and selfish thoughts. We are to ask God for forgiveness and rely on His direction about what we should do about each matter. We can then go to sleep with a clearness of conscience that will likely be a whole new experience for the addict and alcoholic.

consider — think about
divorced — removed
employ — put to use
faculties — minds
assurance — promise of success
plane — level
motives — purposes

On awakening, *let us think about the twenty-four hours ahead. We consider our plans for the day. Before we begin, we ask God to direct our thinking, especially asking that it be divorced from self pity, dishonest or self-seeking motives. Under these conditions we can employ our mental faculties with assurance, for, after all, God gave us brains to use. Our thought life will be placed on a much higher plane when our thinking is cleared of wrong motives.*[21]

When we wake up in the morning, we are instructed to think about the day ahead. We do this automatically, whether we are aware of it or not. But the *Big Book* tells us that before we begin to plan our day that we are to pray. We are told to ask God for His help so that our thinking will be unselfish and God-directed in all our activities that we plan for that day. We can now think about our activities and make plans without the obstruction of self-centeredness that has controlled our lives for so long. The *Big Book* assures us that we will be able to trust these thoughts and we will learn to do so when our motives are to please God and to help others.

In thinking about our day we may face indecision. We may not be able to determine which course to take. Here we ask God for inspiration, an intuitive thought, or a decision. We relax and take it easy. We don't struggle. We are often surprised how the right answers come after we have tried this for a while. What used to be

determine	decide
course	way
inspiration	guidance
intuitive	instinctive
hunch	guess
gradually	slowly over a period of time
presumption	guess
absurd	silly, foolish

the hunch or the occasional inspiration gradually becomes a working part of the mind. Being still inexperienced and having just made conscious contact with God, it is not probable that we are going to be inspired at all times. We might pay for this presumption in all sorts of absurd actions and ideas. Nevertheless, we find that our thinking will, as time passes, be more and more on the plane of inspiration. We come to rely on it.[22]

Many times as we plan our day we will not be able to make a decision. We are not to struggle in making our choices. We pray to God to lead us in the direction that He would have us choose. We are relying on God to guide our thoughts and our actions in every area of our life. Prayer is about contact, not necessarily answers. We will likely make mistakes due to our inexperience, but we are promised as we continue to grow in our prayer life that we will come to depend upon and to trust our own thinking as it aligns with God's guidance for all areas of our lives.

We usually conclude the period of meditation with a prayer that we be shown all through

conclude	end

the day what our next step is to be, that we be given whatever we need to take care of such problems. We ask especially for freedom from self-will, and are careful to make no request for ourselves only. We may ask for ourselves, however, if others will be helped. We are careful never to pray for our own selfish ends. Many of us have wasted a lot of time doing that and it doesn't work. You can easily see why.[23]

We asked God to guide our thinking when we woke up and we have asked Him for direction when we have faced indecision in planning our day. Now we conclude our morning meditation with more prayer for God to direct our thoughts and our actions in all we do. The purpose of prayer is to seek God's will, not to change it. Too often, we make the mistake of seeking God's approval for our own selfish plans rather than for His will.

To make no requests for ourselves only is a valuable piece of advice. It is easy to cover up our selfish motives with seemingly good intentions.

circumstances — conditions
warrant — are called for
emphasize — stress
rabbi — Jewish teacher
agitated — stirred up

If circumstances warrant, we ask our wives or friends to join us in morning meditation. If we belong to a religious denomination which requires a definite morning devotion, we attend to that also. If not members of religious bodies, we sometimes select a few set prayers which emphasize the principles we have been discussing. There are many helpful books also. Suggestions about these may be obtained from one's priest, minister, or rabbi. Be quick to see where religious people are right. Make use of what they offer.[24]

Nothing in the suggestions given for prayer and meditation should interfere with traditions of our existing religious beliefs. We may want our wife, family, or others to join us in our morning devotions. Reading materials such as the Bible or daily meditation books can benefit our spiritual growth. Memorizing or reading set prayers that are consistent with the spiritual principles of the Twelve Steps may also be helpful. If we are unfamiliar with these materials, we can ask for advice from someone who is experienced.

As we go through the day we pause when agitated or doubtful, and ask for the right thought or action. We constantly remind ourselves we are no longer running the show, humbly saying to ourselves many times each day "Thy will be done." We are then in much less danger of excitement, fear, anger, worry, self-pity, or foolish decisions. We become much more efficient. We do not tire so easily, for we are not burning up energy foolishly as we did when we were trying to arrange life to suit ourselves.[25]

> **arrange** — set up

We have asked God to direct our thinking and our actions for the day. Because we began our day with prayer and meditation, we can now face the world relying on all-powerful God rather than our self-centered and selfish nature. We no longer have to make decisions based on emotions and feelings but our decisions can now be grounded in God's truth.

When we feel irritated or upset by something or someone, we are instructed to stop and pray. This is the point where Step Ten and Step Eleven interact. Bill Wilson writes, *"It is a spiritual axiom that every time we are disturbed, no matter what the cause, there is something wrong with us."*[26]

> **axiom** — true fact

Step Ten has instructed us to watch for selfishness, dishonesty, resentment, and fears that indicate we are slipping back into our old way of thinking and to ask God at once to remove whatever is blocking us off from Him. When we are disturbed, we are now able to identify these defects of character in ourselves and are willing to ask God to remove them if we stop and seek God's guidance rather than react on emotions or feelings about the situation or the individual.

The *Big Book* promises as a result of putting these methods into practice, we will then be in less danger of stressful situations and we will have more energy to accomplish things that we could never seem to do before. We will be much more efficient when our focus is on God being in control of our daily lives.

It works — it really does.[27]

The *Big Book* has emphasized the truth that playing God in our own lives didn't work. Now that we have been willing to follow the directions and work the steps of the program, we have experienced the solution that was promised. We have found a way to live that allows God to be God in our lives. We are now learning to live out this truth. Playing God in our own lives doesn't work!

We alcoholics are undisciplined. So we let God discipline us in the simple way we have just outlined.[28]

Most of us have spent years trying to control and manage our own lives. We have now seen the hopelessness of living this way and have asked God to change us. We must be willing to ask God to take control of our lives each day. The very life of every real alcoholic and addict depends upon our willingness to obey spiritual principles. Compliance to these principles is a life and death matter for us.

If he deviates too far, the penalty is sure and swift; he sickens and dies.[29]

But this is not all. There is action and more action. "Faith without works is dead." The next chapter is entirely devoted to Step Twelve.[30]

Praying and meditating each day do not necessarily make me feel better. The unmistakable outcome of unselfish prayer and meditation will always be seen in how we treat others in our daily life.

We now have a message of experience to carry and an unselfish purpose for doing so. Chapter Seven tells us how to carry this message to others and Chapters Eight through Eleven instruct us in how to practice these principles in our lives as we grow in our relationship with God.

Remember, an alcoholic or addict is either growing spiritually or getting ready to use. A spiritual awakening is the result of working these steps and recovery is the result of spiritual growth.

To Love and Be Loved

I felt as though I was being punished by God in His allowing me to continue to suffer the living hell that seemed to be my life.

I had led a wild life as a young alcoholic and drug user and that stage that many go through had turned into a nightmare. I couldn't ever seem to wake up. I needed pills to go to sleep if I was able to sleep at all and more pills to function through the next day. Opiates had control of my life and I was surely dying and welcomed it.

I had tried stopping before. Actually, that was only when my supply ran out and I would suffer so badly from withdrawal symptoms, delirium tremens, severe anxiety, and sleeplessness, that I would inevitably wake up in the hospital having suffered another grand mal seizure. Lack of oxygen to my brain would prevent me from remembering my own birthday, my address, members of my own family, and sometimes even my own name. I have little or no memory of many months and even years of my own adult life.

I would often drink when the pills ran out and if that didn't work, I would turn to meth. Life was a nightmare that I couldn't seem to wake up from.

I had become a mother at the age of 35 and I was terrible at it. My needs always had to come before my daughter's because if I didn't have my fix, I could not care for her anyway. She spent most of her time with relatives because I was either too high to function or was too busy looking to get high. My life was unbearable any way that I turned.

I found a way out of that life one day when I was standing in a court room facing a local judge and certain incarceration for my fourth DUI. That judge suggested that I look into a place called Church Army Branson before he passed sentence.

I checked myself into a local psych ward to be medically detoxed off of the opiates. I then moved into one of the sober living houses for women that Church Army had. It was then I attended the Common Solution Recovery Classes that they offered. Still miserable and suffering both physically and mentally, I saw myself in that cycle of addiction that they drew up on that board. I had known for twenty years that I was an alcoholic and an addict. What I did not realize until that day was that there was hope for someone like me. They told me that I could recover. As bad as my life had become, I too could have a new start and a new way of life.

I willingly followed the directions as they instructed me to do. I discovered in the working of those steps that I had been blocked off from receiving what God wanted me to have by my own resentments and fears and selfishness. It was hard to look at, but when I did, I was opened up to receive the gift of sobriety and a new way of living free of the obsession to use alcohol and drugs.

I did not receive my spiritual awakening at once. I faced my legal issues and incredibly avoided going to prison. I have had to face my past and am making up for my mistakes and probably will be for a long time. But even those experiences have been rewarding for me.

But the most amazing thing though is that my daughter and I have been reunited. We have a beautiful home and I have discovered the true meaning of being a loving mother to her.

I thank God everyday for that judge who led me to Church Army and the Common Solution Recovery Program which, in turn, has led me to meeting the God who loves me and doesn't want to punish me. I love being able to share God's love and to offer the hope and promise of recovery to those who need it.

I am most blessed to have found a way to truly love and to be loved in return.

> It is one of the most beautiful compensations
> of this life that no man can sincerely try to
> help another without helping himself.
> — Ralph Waldo Emerson

STEP TWELVE

CARRY *THIS* MESSAGE

*For if an alcoholic failed to perfect and enlarge
his spiritual life through work and self-sacrifice
for others, he could not survive the certain
trials and low spots ahead.*[1]

*Having **had** a spiritual awakening as **the** result of **these** steps* . . . the event of recovery has occurred naturally as the result of the working of the steps of the program of Alcoholics Anonymous. Somewhere in the action we have taken based on our willingness to follow the specific, precise, and clear-cut directions of the *Big Book* and an ongoing willingness to practice these spiritual principles in our own lives, we will have experienced a personality change sufficient to recover. The obsession to use alcohol and/or drugs has been removed by God and we have become one of the many alcoholics and addicts who are recovered.

We have been given this gift of freedom from alcohol and drugs by God and God alone. So we are now qualified and are even compelled to carry this message to others who are suffering in their addiction as we once were. In fact, we are not only eligible to carry this message, but to do so will provide the promise that we will continue to grow in our own spiritual walk with God.

Practical experience shows that nothing will so much insure immunity from drinking as intensive work with other alcoholics. It works when other activities fail. This is our

practical — matter of fact
insure — guarantee
immunity — protection
intensive — strenuous

twelfth suggestion: Carry this message to other alcoholics! You can help when no one else can. You can secure their confidence where others fail. Remember they are very ill.[2]

The founders and early members of Alcoholics Anonymous discovered from the very beginning that helping other alcoholics to find a way out of the addictive lifestyle was essential to their own recovery. Bill Wilson was able to stay sober by working with Dr. Bob. Bill and Dr. Bob immediately began to work with AA Number Three, a lawyer named Bill Dodson who was undergoing detoxification in St. Thomas Hospital in Akron, Ohio.[3]

Working with others, carrying the message of what God has done for you and in you as the result of working the Twelve Steps, is the foundation of every successful recovery. The original draft of the *Big Book* as it was written in 1938 stressed that the alcoholic suffers from a deadly illness and that working with others is effective when prayer, mediation, and self-examination fall short. Note the words that were removed from the original manuscript of the *Big Book*.

Practical experience shows that nothing will so much insure your own immunity from drinking as intensive work with other alcoholics. It works when other **spiritual** activities fail. This is our twelfth suggestion: Carry this message to other alcoholics! You can help when no one else can. You can secure their confidence when others fail. Remember they are **fatally** ill.[4]

Our very lives, as ex-problem drinkers, depend upon our constant thought of others and how we may meet their needs.[5]

The individual who possesses the three pieces of information necessary to recover (problem, solution, and how to find the solution) now has a challenging responsibility to pass this information on to those who have not yet found a way out. Alcoholism, we have learned, is a life and death struggle and we have experienced a solution that has worked in us and will do the same in others if they are offered it as we once were.

Life will take on new meaning. To watch people recover, to see them help others, to watch loneliness vanish, to see a fellowship grow up about you, to have a host of friends — this is an experience that you must not miss. We know that you will not want to miss it. Frequent contact with newcomers and with each other is the bright spot of our lives.[6]

The founders of Alcoholics Anonymous experienced this need as a result of working the steps. When we came seeking help, we were without hope; we had nothing to offer others and felt alone in the world where it seemed no one understood us. Now we have experienced a spiritual awakening as the result of working these Twelve Steps and we want to tell the world about it. People who have been helped feel a need to help others. When Bill Wilson's spiritual advisor, the Reverend Sam Shoemaker addressed the 20th anniversary convention of AA in St. Louis, Missouri, in 1955, he spoke of just that need.

"As I looked out over that crowd of five thousand in Kiel Auditorium in St. Louis, I said to myself, *Would that the Church were like this — ordinary men and women with great need who have found a great Answer, and do not hesitate to make it known wherever they can — a trained army of enthusiastic, humble, human workers whose efforts make life a different thing for other people!*"

This need to be in contact with others is the foundation upon which the fellowship of AA was born. These meetings were designed to be a place where a newcomer could come and get help with recovery. He or she could come to a meeting, find help in identifying the problem, be offered the solution, and be given assistance in the working of the steps. However, the fellowship was never meant to replace God as the solution. The *Big Book* warns us of this danger of using the human resource of meetings as a substitute for working the steps of the program.

The feeling of having shared in a common peril is one element in the powerful cement which binds us. But that in itself would never have held us together as we are now joined.[7]

We have experienced a common solution and that is the message that we are to carry to other still suffering alcoholics and addicts. That is the message the *Big Book* carries; that is the only message that we can carry. In fact, we believe that to achieve the sobriety and serenity that God has planned for each of us, we must carry this message, the message found in the *Big Book*, to the newcomer. This is working Step Twelve. There are many opportunities to serve in the meeting rooms of a Twelve-Step Group. However, this service work should never be confused with or used as a substitution for working Step Twelve; that is, "carrying this message."

The only two requirements for carrying this message is to have had the problem and to have experienced the solution, a spiritual awakening, as the result of these steps. The alcoholic or addict who has "had a spiritual awakening as the result of these steps" is uniquely qualified to carry this message. We cannot transmit what we haven't got.[8] We are to carry this message to those still suffering both in and out of AA meetings.

"How do I carry the message?" is a commonly asked question by alcoholics who have just had a spiritual awakening.

Chapter Seven of the *Big Book* is written to provide us with a general guideline to working with others and shares the experience of early AA's in working one-on-one with others.

Meetings, study groups, and conventions are never meant to replace the satisfaction and spiritual growth that we experience in helping another human being find their way out of the "cave" of addiction to drugs and alcohol. The experience of our own past is invaluable in working with others. We are the only persons who can honestly say, "I know how you feel."

But the ex-problem drinker who has found this solution, who is properly armed with facts about himself, can generally win the entire confidence of another alcoholic in a few hours. Until such an understanding can be reached, little or nothing can be accomplished.

That the man who is making the approach has had the same difficulty, that he obviously knows what he is talking about, that his whole deportment shouts at the

> deportment — behavior

new prospect that he is a man with a real answer, that he has no attitude of Holier Than Thou, nothing whatever except the sincere desire to be helpful; that there are no dues to pay, no lectures to be endured — these are the conditions we have found most effective.[9]

Ministers and doctors are competent and you can learn much from them if you wish, but it happens that because of your own drinking experience you can be uniquely useful to other alcoholics. So cooperate; never criticize. To be helpful is our only aim.[10]

The *Big Book* was first published in 1939 and much has changed in the world of alcoholism. Treatment centers abound, and though not affiliated with AA, they have certainly affected it in varying degrees. Many more females and young people now come to AA seeking sobriety. They bring the problems of new and powerful substances into the midst

of the fellowship. The growth in methamphetamine and prescription pill addiction has reached epidemic proportions in
many areas. However, the best advice on how to carry this
message to the individual is still contained in Chapter Seven
of the *Big Book*. Face-to-face meetings with the alcoholic and
addict are still necessary, whether they are in treatment or
elsewhere.

Find out all you can about the prospect from those closest to him if
possible. Don't waste time trying to persuade them to stop drinking
or using.[11]

Put yourself in their place. Ask yourself what approach would
reach you if you were in their condition.[12]

Don't deal with them when they are too drunk or too high.[13]

Never force yourself or allow others to force you upon the prospect.
Place the book where they can see it. Tell the family not to be over-
anxious.[14]

See them alone if possible. Tell them of your own drinking and
drug use. Don't talk about the solution at this time.[15]

Describe yourself as an alcoholic or addict.[16]

Share your story of your struggles to stop; talk about the mental
twist that always led to using.[17]

Dwell on the hopeless feature of the problem. Continue to talk
about your own experience and battles to stop. Be careful not to
brand him or her as an alcoholic or addict.[18]

Continue to speak of the problem as an illness of the body and
mind.[19]

Let them ask you how you got well. Tell them exactly what hap-
pened to you. Stress the spiritual feature freely. Make it clear that
they do not have to agree with your conception of God. Tell them

that they only need to be willing to believe in a Power greater than themselves.[20]

Don't evangelize![21]

Outline the program of action contained in the Big Book. *Tell them that your attempt to help them is vital to your own recovery. Explain that they may be helping you more than you are helping them. Make it clear that they are under no obligation to you.*[22]

Do not argue. Offer them a copy of the Big Book *if they are interested.*[23]

Don't stay if you are asked to leave. Don't talk down to them. Lay out the steps for their inspection. Show them how the program worked for you. Offer them friendship and offer to help if they want help.[24]

Ask them to read the Big Book *after you leave.*[25]

Encourage them to follow their own plan to find a spiritual method of recovery. Share again that the steps worked for you.[26]

Don't be discouraged if they don't respond. Don't chase them.[27]

If you see them again and are prepared to go through with the program, offer your help. Don't insist on being their Fifth Step partner.[28]

Help them financially as long as you don't deprive your family in doing so. Use discretion. Don't allow them to use you as a banker or impose on you for a place to stay or a job. This may aid in their destruction rather than their recovery.[29]

Do not neglect their family. Offer the family the program of recovery.[30]

Do not put your work on a service plane. Stress to him/her that dependence upon God must come ahead of everything for them to recover.[31]

Burn the idea into the consciousness of every man that he can get well regardless of anyone. The only condition is that he trust God and clean house.[32]

Help each other on your path of spiritual progress, putting yourselves in God's hands. Follow God's guidance and direction.[33]

Don't participate in his/her family quarrels.[34]

Share your own success, if possible.[35]

Never show intolerance or hatred of drinking as an institution or drug addicts and alcoholics as a whole.[36]

These are guiding principles that still prove most effective in working with another alcoholic or addict. This transmittal of information has come to be called sponsorship.

The term "sponsor" and "sponsee" are never used in the *Big Book of AA*, but sponsorship has become the common method of passing on the information needed for recovery among individuals. True sponsorship is more than giving rides to meetings or speaking every day on the phone.

Though there is no definition in the *Big Book*, a true sponsor has the singular task of guiding someone through the working of the steps so that they can guide someone else through. Anything apart from this single purpose can be helpful but it is not really sponsoring.

I encourage newcomers who know that they have a problem to ask the potential sponsor if he or she has had a spiritual awakening as the result of working these steps. If they say "No" or offer some other method of recovery, I tell them to walk away and find someone else to sponsor them. The person who has experienced the solution as the result of working the steps will be receptive to anyone who asks them to help.

I am often confronted with "There is more to Step Twelve than carrying the message" comments. I agree that "to practice these principles in all our affairs is necessary." We must practice these principles at home, at work, at all times, in and out of the rooms of AA. However, if I am watching for selfishness and other defects and asking God to remove them when they arise; if I am making amends for my past and current behavior as directed by God; if I am doing all I can to live and grow in relationship with Him through self-examination, prayer, meditation, and working with others, I will naturally be practicing the principles of the Twelve Steps in all my affairs.

Working with others is not an option if we are to grow spiritually. The source of true happiness and purpose in our lives will only be found in working with others. God sent someone to help us find a way out of the pit of addiction and He has given each of us a job to do the same.

We have been speaking to you of serious, sometimes tragic things. We have been dealing with alcohol in its worst aspect. But we aren't a glum lot. If newcomers could see no joy or fun in our existence, they wouldn't want it. We absolutely insist on enjoying life.

So we think that cheerfulness and laughter make for usefulness. Outsiders are sometimes shocked when we burst into merriment over a seemingly tragic experience out of the past. But why shouldn't we laugh? We have recovered and been given the power to help others.[37]

"WE HAVE RECOVERED, AND HAVE BEEN GIVEN THE POWER TO HELP OTHERS."

Once an alcoholic had fallen into a deep hole and could not find an escape. The sides were steep and slick and he could not climb out. After trying and failing for many hours, in desperation, he began to shout for help.

A lawyer was walking by and heard his cry. The lawyer cautiously approached the edge of the pit and asked what he could do to help. The alcoholic said, "Help me get out of this hole!" The lawyer said, "I don't know how to help, but if you ever do get out, give me a call and we will sue the person who dug that hole and left it uncovered." With that, he threw his business card down into the hole and walked away.

The alcoholic began to cry out louder than before and a doctor heard him. The doctor leaned over from the edge and asked him if he was hurt and what could he do for him. Again, the alcoholic begged for help to get out of the hole. The doctor told him, "I can't get you out but I can give you a prescription to ease your pain. Call me for an appointment if you ever do get out of there." He wrote the prescription, threw it down into the hole and walked away.

The next person to answer his call was a preacher. He listened to the alcoholic ask him for help, shook his head and tossed his Bible down into the hole. He said, "I will pray for you every day until you can come to church." With that, he turned and left.

The man in the hole gave up on getting help and resigned himself to being stuck in that hole until he starved to death. About that time, a *recovered* alcoholic passed by and looked down into the hole.

The alcoholic cried out, "Help me. I'm trapped here and I can't get out!" Without a word the recovered alcoholic jumped down into the hole with him. The drunk said, "What are you doing? Now we are both stuck here."

But the recovered alcoholic calmly looked at him and said, "That's okay. I've been in this hole before and I know the way out."

There is recovery, there is a way out. No matter how hopeless things may seem, there is help for the hopeless and lost.

Rarely have we seen a person fail. . . .[38]

Broken Life Mended, Lost Dreams Restored

One of my first memories was of my parents divorcing after years of bitter fighting and abuse. I was five years old and was with my mom who pretty much handed me off to my grandparents to raise. She was a real alcoholic who supplied my first joint and beer at age seven. We lived in a small suburb of Chicago. Our house was filled with all kinds of animals; dogs, horses, ducks, pigs, and over 30 goats at any given time. I spent most of my schooldays living with the embarrassment and shame that I was not like the other kids.

Strangely enough, instead of feeling bitterness and anger toward her, I felt I was responsible to take care of her. I was obsessed with protecting her from the men she was with, her drunk driving, and her many threats of suicide. I took my caretaker role very seriously and using her drugs and alcohol became the way that I could cope and seemingly control the chaos that surrounded me. By the age of 13, I was drinking to the point of blackouts and awakening in my own urine.

The more I drank, the more in control I felt. I liked running my own life and thought that I was very good at it. I forged my birth certificate and got a job in the food service industry. At age 14 I bought a car, and a year later left my mother and was living on my own.

My new life consisted of working so that I could feel important, saving money so I could feel secure, and drinking and smoking so I could feel in control. All in all, my life was pretty good and my self-reliance was seemingly working.

I was running my own life, paying my own way and was doing great. Despite the constant blackouts, the auto accidents, and several alcohol related arrests, I continued to feel that I was in charge of my own life and was doing a pretty good job of it.

Sexual relationships came and went and I believed that was just the way people lived. I sometimes sensed that there was something wrong with me, but a few drinks and some drugs soon replaced those feelings of insecurity and doubt with power and control.

This went on for a few years until a near-fatal auto accident led me to begin some kind of soul searching and I began to get involved with psychics, forms of astral projection, astrology, and other self-help methods of seeking. This went on for several years, jumping back and forth from one code of beliefs to another, all the while claiming to be a stone cold atheist.

I had relocated from Chicago and had landed a high-pressure executive position with a large corporation. By now I was drinking for oblivion almost nightly. Another driving drunk charge led me to the point of despair and I cried out for help from a jail cell. The thought came to me, *Go to AA.* I went, and for the first time in my life I felt I was somewhere that I belonged.

I became a full-time member of the fellowship and for two years I felt better . . . as long as I was in those meetings. But the rest of the time I was more miserable than ever. Depression and constant thoughts of suicide were my secret life outside of those meeting rooms where I would put on a smiling face and tell everyone how great my life was.

After two years of sober insanity, I was finally defeated. I took the first step that I had been claiming to have done for those two years. One man in that whole group spoke of "recovery" following the directions of the *Big Book.* He had a peace about him that was sincere and true. I wanted what he had. He simply told me to "Work the steps." After I had inventoried and shared my shortcomings with a trusted friend

I asked God to change me and the results were miraculous and instantaneous.

That was almost two decades ago and I have never had to return to alcohol or drugs for relief from any situation that I have run into in my life. The Twelve Steps are the path to God that worked for me and God is the God who sobered me and saved me from the life that He never intended for me to live.

Today I use the tools that I was given, and His presence in my heart is so overwhelming that sometimes I cannot contain it, and my life and the life of those around me is very, very good. Some days I turn away from Him and back to relying on myself to run my life and life becomes difficult.

But the steps have taught me that He is always there waiting for me to come back to Him. He loves me and allows me the privilege of sharing His message of hope and recovery with those who are where I once was.

Today I have found security and hope and peace and meaning in a life based on spiritual principles and a love for God. He will never let you down.

For all that has been, thanks.
For all that shall be, yes.
— Dag Hammarskjold

CONCLUSION

Thus we grow.[1]

G.K. Chesterton was a famous novelist and essayist at the turn of the 20th century. He and several literary figures were once asked what book they would prefer to have with them if they were stranded on a desert island.

"*The Complete Works of Shakespeare,*" said one writer.

"I would choose the Bible," said another.

"How about you?" they asked Chesterton.

Without hesitation, he replied, "I would choose a book like *Thomas's Guide to Practical Shipbuilding.*"

Chesterton undoubtedly made his choice of book based on the circumstances in which he was placed. The *Big Book of Alcoholics Anonymous* is just such a guide for those stranded on the desert island of alcoholism and addiction. And *We Have Recovered* is a reminder for all of us that there is a common solution, that there is a way out and a way off of that island.

We have covered much in these pages. It is our best amateur attempt to present the same program that is taught each week to hundreds of men and women in our classrooms who are seeking a real solution to the plague of alcoholism and drug addictions.

It is in no way an attempt to alter or change the words of the *Big Book*. Like most fundamentalists in and out of AA, we consider the Twelve Steps and the first 164 pages of the *Big*

193

Book along with the "Doctor's Opinion" to be God's personal gift to every person who has found recovery in its message. Every one of us who has picked up the *Big Book* and used it as a guide to get off of that island knows first-hand the miracle of the grace of God.

Simple, but not easy . . . that is what we were told.[2] And was that ever so true when we tried it. The program of recovery contained in the *Big Book* is sometimes said to be tried and found difficult. I see many more who find the program difficult and not try it at all. And the results of seeking an easier, softer way are often tragic for the real alcoholic and addict.

At our recovery center, the walls are covered with plaques commemorating those who have finished one of our year-long programs.[3] Most worked the Steps out of the *Big Book* as they were presented in the Common Solution Recovery Program. One section of the wall, however, is for men and women who met untimely deaths directly or indirectly caused by their addictions — suicide, murder by a drug dealer, alcohol poisoning, and drug overdoses, among others. The thing that they shared in common apart from an early death was the fact that each of them had left the Twelve Step program of recovery for an easier, softer one. They all had made the decision but had never taken the action.

The Twelve Steps are surely simple. But never easy.

When we arrived, we were first given the information to make a mental conclusion of what our problem is. However, like most people who had been taught to rely on themselves, the admission of powerlessness did not come easy. We found that resolve of the will alone could not overcome our obsession to drink and use; we couldn't just decide to stop drinking and drugging. Many of us have paid a high price to discover that truth.

Then we were told that we must be willing to believe in a Power greater than ourselves. That we must make a second mental conclusion that there is a Power that exists outside of our human resources that can reach into our mind and remove the deadly obsession. We looked around us and saw changed lives and smiling faces, and our minds were opened ever so slightly to the possibility that there was hope for a new life.

We were being led by loving friends that we sensed cared for us for some reason that we didn't yet understand. But they helped us to make that decision to seek the solution that was offered and that they had found. People were speaking to us about a God who cares personally about each of us, so we said the prayer that they told us to say and we felt better.

Now we thought that we needed to rest after making those two exhausting mental conclusions followed by the hard work of the decision. These people who seem to know what they are talking about told us we were now to begin looking at our past; who we hated, what we were afraid of, and how we have hurt people. No time to rest, no breaks or time off. They told us to begin to write at once. And they stood with us and told us that there is no such thing as a bad question. Simple? Yes. Easy? No way.

We are told not to stop on the Fourth Step and were urged to find a Fifth Step partner. We came to that partner afraid of what they were going to think about us when they heard our secrets, but we remained willing to go through with the whole process. Turns out, they had done many of the things that we are so ashamed of themselves and in some cases much more.

Then we spent an hour looking at what we had done so far. We talked with God (a novel experience for most of us) and to ourselves, and something happened. We began to feel convicted of who and what we are without Him.

Then come those moments of change. We open up a corner of our life to God's forgiving grace and we pray for Him to take charge. And somehow we know that He hears us. An experience that can only be felt and never explained. Different for each of us. But we sense that something great has happened.

Then they show us how to make the decision to live simply, one day at a time, in dependence upon God and His will for us. They give us a way to live so that will happen if we follow the instructions of the *Big Book*. And we now have a purpose.

Just when we think we can kick back and take it easy, they tell us to "Pass it on." We are told to attend meetings and classes and share our experience with the new person who is seeking sobriety. We have been told by many well-meaning people that we need to wait a year before we sponsor anyone. A.A. history and the *Big Book* don't agree with that time-line. Joe McQ of the *Joe and Charlie Big Book Study* once told me, "If an alcoholic or addict is not sponsoring and working with others within the first year of sobriety, chances are they never will." So we look for a newcomer and trust God for the words to say.

Rest assured that there is nothing easy about the program of Alcoholics Anonymous. My grand sponsor used to tap on the cover of his book with his big index finger and say, "This is the toughest God program on the face of the earth, and we have to live it." Then he would smile and say how grateful he was that he got to do just that.

Spiritual growth is a must for the alcoholic or addict. This requires more than attendance at AA meetings and service work. Although both can be good, they are seldom enough. True spiritual growth will come from making amends, watching for self creeping back into my life, along with prayer and meditation. But most of all, as Bill Wilson stated in "Bill's Story" that when all other measures failed, work with another alcoholic would save the day.[4]

There has probably been enough written in *We Have Recovered* to offend just about anyone. But that was never the intention. This book was written to offer help to those still suffering who are living apart from the basic spiritual principles that the *Big Book* offers. That is one of the great things about the Twelve Steps. If I am hurt or upset, I live a program that offers me a way to handle any disagreement.

Time means change, of course. But inevitable change does not alter basic truth. The alcoholic that the *Big Book* was written for is the same. He is now many more she's; they are mixing more exotic substances with the alcohol and dying much more quickly than ever before. They are younger and seeking someone who "speaks their language." However, the basic problem remains the obsession of the mind coupled with the allergy of the body.

Out of respect for the Traditions of Alcoholics Anonymous, some meetings are closed and should remain that way. But for the addict and the alcoholic-addict the Steps work exactly the same and many of the meetings have been unselfishly opened up to all. The current member can then choose to not attend, should he so desire, and all should be pleased. And the newcomer should be respectfully taught the Traditions and to stay out of closed meetings unless he or she expresses a desire to stop drinking.[5]

The results of a life addicted to alcohol and drugs haven't changed; the basic alcoholic still has the same problem of mind and body regardless of age or gender. The solution has not changed.

God is the same today as He was when the universe or the church or Alcoholics Anonymous were created. He is the only solution that has ever worked for the real alcoholic and He is the only provider of miracles. He is the only answer to unsolvable problems.

He has given us a way out of our messed-up lives, regardless of how far we have fallen or how ugly life has become. Junkie or juicer. Meth or martinis. Chemicals or cocktails. He is there; He has always been there.

Much has not been said. We have tried to limit the extent of *We Have Recovered* to reach the newcomer who has never worked the steps. Therefore, there is little mention of sponsorship or how to be a good Fifth Step partner. Little of the extensive and fascinating history of AA has been touched on. I recommend books by Wally P. and Dick B., among others who masterly cover that topic. The Joe McQ book *Carry This Message* is among the best that can be found on sponsorship. All are well researched and filled with foundational truths, separated from many of the myths that surround Alcoholics Anonymous.

Truth means all things to the dying addict and alcoholic. We have found that truth confirmed by experience results in absolute certainty. The man who loved me the most told me the truth. He told me that I was going to die an ugly death and there was nothing I could do about it. He cared more about whether I lived or died than whether I liked him or what he was saying. He spoke the truth in love.

Nevertheless, the experience had to be mine. I had only to be willing to believe and act on that willingness. And when the action led to change, I became convinced that he had spoken the truth. I now live a life of certainty that if the Twelve Steps of Alcoholics Anonymous are worked in order and following the specific, precise and clear-cut instructions from the *Big Book*, then practiced as a way of life, recovery is a certainty for everyone willing to do just that. It never fails.

We Have Recovered is our modest attempt to help those who suffer in a life consumed by alcohol and drugs; to show them and their families a way out of that cave, a way off of that desert island. Nothing is new in the sense of never having before existed; there are no new answers here. Many have gone much deeper into these topics than we have.

But none have gone with a greater love than we have been given to feel for the lost and dying addict and alcoholic. The fire in us is real and blazes with a sincere desire to help others, and if there are two or ten or a hundred who can light their own candle from the fire that burns within these pages, our lives have come to mean something and all thanks are to be given to the only God who is the only good.

May He bless you and be with you on your journey to recovery as He has blessed so many of us on ours.

Endnotes

Prefix

1. *Alcoholics Anonymous (Big Book of AA), 4th edition* (Alcoholics Anonymous World Services, Inc., 2001), p. xiii.

Introduction

1. *Big Book of AA*, p. 17, para. 3
2. Ibid., p. xx, para. 1 of the Fourth Edition. "Of the alcoholics who came to A.A. and really tried, 50% got sober at once and remained that way; 25% sobered up after some relapses. . . ."
3. Ibid, p. xvii, para. 4: "The fledgling society, which had been nameless, now began to be called Alcoholics Anonymous, from the title of its own book."
4. Bill Wilson article, *A.A. Grapevine*, February 1958.
5. *Big Book of AA*, p. 122, para. 1.
6. Humanism is defined as a system of thought that is based on the values, characteristics, and behavior that are believed to be best in human beings, rather than on any supernatural authority.
7. *Big Book of AA*, p. 53, para. 3.
8. Twelve and Twelve, p. 15, para. 3.
9. Edwin Throckmorton Thacher was the boyhood friend who carried the message of the Oxford Group to Bill Wilson with great care and dedication — that recovery from alcoholism was possible using spiritual principles, but only if it was combined with practical actions.
10. *Big Book of AA*, p. 13, para. 5: "My friend promised when these things were done I would enter into a new relationship with my Creator; that I would have the elements of a way of living which answered all my problems."

Step One — What Is the Problem?

1. *Big Book of AA*, p. 8.
2. Ibid., p. xxvi, para. 1.
3. Ibid., p. 7, para. 1.
4. Ibid., p. xxv, para. 1.
5. Ibid., p. xxvi, para. 1.
6. *American Heritage Dictionary of the English Language*, 4th edition (Boston, MA: Houghton Mifflin, 2009).
7. *Big Book of AA*, p. xxx, para. 5.
8. Ibid., p. 21, para. 2.
9. Ibid., p. 22, para. 5.
10. Ibid., p. 30, para. 3.
11. Ibid., p. 30, para. 4.
12. Ibid., p. 31, para. 1.
13. Ibid., p. 33, para. 2.
14. Ibid., p. 34, para. 3.
15. Ibid., p. xxvi, para. 5.
16. Ibid., p. 23, para. 1.
17. Ibid., p. 23, para. 2.
18. Ibid., p. 30, para. 1.
19. Ibid., p. 30, para. 2.
20. Ibid., p. 33, para. 2.
21. Ibid., p. 33, para. 3.
22. Ibid., p. xxvi, para. 5.
23. Ibid., p. 35, para. 1.
24. Ibid., p. 36, para. 3.
25. Ibid., p. 37, para. 2.

26. Ibid., p. 41, para. 3.
27. Ibid., p. 3, para. 2.
28. Ibid., p. 4, para. 2.
29. Ibid., p. 5, para. 2.
30. Ibid., p. 7, para. 1.
31. Ibid., p. 8, para. 2.
32. Ibid., p. 7, para. 2.
33. Ibid., p. 7, para. 4.

Step Two — What Is *Not* the Solution

1. *Big Book*, p. 60.
2. Ibid., p. 17, para. 3.
3. Ibid., p. 28, para. 3.
4. Ibid., p. 21, para. 2.
5. Ibid., p. 23, para. 5.
6. Ibid., p. 30, para. 1.
7. Ibid., p. 30, para. 4.
8. Ibid., p. 31, para. 1.
9. Ibid., p. 34, para. 1.
10. Ibid., p. 35, para. 3.
11. Ibid., p. 20, para. 5.
12. Ibid., p. 21, para. 2.
13. Ibid., p. 41, para. 3.
14. Ibid., p. 60, para. 3.
15. Ibid., p. 44, para. 4.
16. Ibid., p. 45, para. 1.
17. Ibid., p. 30, para. 2.
18. Ibid., p. 43, para. 4.

Step Two — What Is the Solution

1. *Big Book of AA*, p. 12
2. Ibid., p. 44, para. 1.
3. Ibid., p. 31, para. 4.
4. Ibid., p. 33, para. 2.
5. Ibid., p. 45, para. 3.
6. Ibid., p. 28, para. 4.
7. Ibid., p. 29, para. 3.
8. Ibid., p. 50, para. 2.
9. Ibid., p. 50, para. 3.
10. Ibid., p. 44, para. 2.
11. Ibid., p. 47, para. 2.
12. Ibid., p. 567–568.
13. Ibid., appendix II.
14. Ibid., p. 25, para. 4.

15. Ibid., p. 59.
16. Ibid., p. 59.
17. Ibid., p. 47, para. 2.
18. Ibid., p. 12, para. 3.
19. Ibid., p. 12, para. 5.

Step Three — Decision

1. *Big Book of AA*, p. 60.
2. Ibid., p. 60, para. 2.
3. Original Manuscript of the *Big Book*, 1938.
4. *Big Book of AA*, p. 60, para. 3.
5. Ibid., p. 60, para. 4.
6. Ibid., p. 62, para. 2.
7. Ibid., p. 62, para. 3.
8. Ibid., p. 23, para. 1.
9. Ibid., p. 62, para. 3.
10. Ibid., p. 60, para. 3.
11. Ibid.
12. Ibid., p. 63, para. 2.
13. Ibid., p. 23.
14. Ibid., p. 62.
15. Ibid., p. 63.
16. Ibid., p. 63, para. 3.
17. Ibid., p. 35, para. 3.
18. Ibid., p. 14, para. 7.
19. Ibid., p. 63, para. 3.

Step Four — The Written Inventory

1. *Big Book of AA*, p. 13.
2. Ibid., p. 63, last para.
3. Ibid., p. 58, last para.
4. Ibid., p. 64, para. 2.
5. Ibid., p. 55, para. 2.
6. Ibid., p. 55, para. 3.
7. Ibid., p. 64, para. 2.

Step Four — Resentments

1. *Big Book of AA*, p. 64.
2. Ibid., p. 66, para. 1.
3. Ibid., p. 64, para. 4.
4. Ibid.
5. Ibid., p. 65, para. 3.
6. Ibid.
7. Ibid., p. 66, para. 2.

8. Ibid., p. 66, para. 3.
9. Ibid., p. 66, para. 4.
10. Ibid., p. 66, para. 5.
11. Ibid., p. 67, para. 2.
12. Ibid., p. 67, para. 3.
13. Ibid., p. 23.
14. Ibid., p. 62.
15. Ibid., p. 63.

Step Four — Fears

1. *Big Book of AA*, p. 67.
2. Ibid., p. 67, para. 4.
3. Ibid., p. 68, para. 2.
4. Ibid.,
5. Ibid., p. 68, para. 4.
6. Ibid., p. 23.
7. Ibid., p. 62.
8. Ibid., p. 63.

Step Four — Sex Conduct

1. *Big Book of AA*, p. 68, para. 5.
2. Ibid.
3. Ibid., p. 69, para. 1.
4. Ibid., p. 69, para. 2.
5. Ibid., p. 69, para. 3.
6. Ibid., p. 69, para. 4.
7. Ibid., p. 69, para. 5.
8. Ibid., p. 70, para. 2.
9. Ibid., p. 70, para. 3.
10. Ibid., p. 23.
11. Ibid., p. 62.
12. Ibid., p. 63.
13. Ibid., p. 70, para. 4.
14. Ibid., p. 70, para. 5.
15. This was only a beginning. *Big Book*, p. 63, para. 3.
16. . . . you have made a good beginning. *Big Book*, p. 71, para. 1.

Step Five — Discussing Ourselves with Another Person

1. *Big Book of AA*, p. 13, para. 3.
2. Ibid., p. 72, para. 1.
3. Ibid., p. 72, para. 2.

4. Ibid., The Twelve Steps and Twelve Traditions, p. 61.
5. Ibid., p. 96, para. 2.
6. Ibid., p. 73, para. 5.
7. Ibid., p. 74, para. 2.
8. Ibid., p. 74, para. 3.
9. Ibid., p. 75, para. 2.
10. Ibid., p. 75, para. 3.
11. Ibid., p. 75, para. 4.

Steps Six and Seven — Change

1. *Big Book of AA*, p. 13.
2. Ibid., p. 64, para. 2.
3. Being all-powerful, God can of course remove anything that blocks us from Him. The question is not "Does He have the power to do so?" but rather we should ask ourselves if we are willing to let Him.
4. *Big Book of AA.*, p. 76, para. 1.
5. Ibid., p. 62, para. 3.
6. Oswald Chambers, *My Utmost for His Highest* (New York: Dodd, Mead & Co., 1935).
7. *Big Book of AA.*, p. 76, para. 2.
8. Ibid., p. 76, para. 2.

Steps Eight and Nine — Amends

1. *Big Book of AA*, p. 13, para. 4.
2. Ibid., p. 76, para. 3.
3. Ibid., p. 68.
4. Ibid., p. 77, para. 3.
5. Ibid., p. 78, para. 3.
6. Ibid., p. 78, para. 4.
7. Ibid., p. 79, para. 3.
8. Ibid., p. 80, para. 5.
9. Ibid., p. 82, para. 3.
10. Ibid., p. 83, para. 3.
11. Ibid., p. 77, para. 1.
12. Ibid., Seventh Step Prayer, p. 76.
13. Chuck Swindoll, *Lamentations*.
14. *Big Book of AA*, p. 77, para. 1.
15. Ibid., p. 77, para. 3.

16. Ibid., p. 79, para. 2.
17. Ibid., p. 58.
18. Ibid., p. 76.
19. Ibid., p. 79, para. 2.
20. Ibid., p. 79, para. 3.
21. Ibid., p. 80, para. 1.
22. Ibid., p. 83, para. 2.
23. Ibid., p. 83, para. 4–p. 84, para. 1.
24. Ibid., Twelve and Twelve, p. 82.

Steps Ten and Eleven — Self-examination, Prayer, and Meditation

1. *Big Book of AA*, p. 13.
2. Ibid., Twelve and Twelve, p. 98, para. 2.
3. Ibid., p. 59.
4. Ibid., p. 84, para. 3.
5. Ibid., p. 8, para. 3; p. 25, para. 2.
6. Ibid., p. 84, para. 4.
7. Ibid., p. 84, para. 4.
8. Ibid., p. 84, para. 4.
9, Ibid., p. 84, para. 4.
10. Ibid., p. 84, para. 4.
11. Ibid., p. 85, para. 1.
12. Ibid., p. 85, para. 1.
13. Ibid., p. 100–103.
14. Ibid., p. 85, para. 1.
15. Ibid., p. 85, para. 1.
16. Ibid., p. 85, para. 1.
17. Ibid., p. 85, para. 2.
18. Ibid., p. 85, para. 3.
19. Ibid., p. 59.
20. Ibid., p. 86, para. 2.
21. Ibid., p. 86, para. 3.
22. Ibid., p. 86, para. 4.
23. Ibid., p. 87, para. 2.
24. Ibid., p. 87.
25. Ibid., p. 87, para. 4.
26. Ibid., Twelve and Twelve, p. 90, para. 3.
27. Ibid., p. 88, para. 2.
28. Ibid., p. 88, para. 3.
29. Ibid., p. 130, para. 2.
30. Ibid., p. 88, para. 4.

Step Twelve — Carry This Message

1. *Big Book of AA*, p. 14, para. 7.
2. Ibid., p. 89, para. 1.
3. Ibid., p., xvii, para. 2, fourth edition.
4. Original Manuscript of the *Big Book*.
5. Ibid., p. 20, para. 1.
6. Ibid., p. 89, para. 2.
7. Ibid., p. 17, para. 2.
8. Ibid., p. 164, para. 3.
9. Ibid., p. 18, para. 4.
10. Ibid., p. 89, para. 3.
11. Ibid., p. 90, para. 1.
12. Ibid., p. 90, para. 2.
13. Ibid., p. 90, para. 3.
14. Ibid., p. 90, para. 4.
15. Ibid., p. 91, para. 4.
16. Ibid., p. 91, para. 5.
17. Ibid., p. 92, para. 1.
18. Ibid., p. 92, para. 2.
19. Ibid., p. 92, para. 3.
20. Ibid., p. 93, para. 1.
21. Ibid., p. 93, para. 2.
22. Ibid., p. 94, para. 2.
23. Ibid., p. 94, para. 3.
24. Ibid., p. 95, para. 1.
25. Ibid., p. 95, para. 3.
26. Ibid., p. 95, para. 4.
27. Ibid., p. 96, para. 1.
28. Ibid., p. 96, para. 2.
29. Ibid., p. 96, para. 3.
30. Ibid., p. 97, para. 4.
31. Ibid., p. 98, para. 2.
32. Ibid., p. 98, para. 3.
33. Ibid., p. 100, para. 2.
34. Ibid., p. 100, para. 3.
35. Ibid., p. 100, para. 4.
36. Ibid., p. 103, para. 2.
37. Ibid., p. 132, para. 2 and 3.
38. Ibid., p. 58, para. 1.

Conclusion

1. *Big Book of AA*, p. 88.
2. Ibid., p. 14, para. 2.
3. Cambridge Project, Peer to Peer Project, Single Mother's Program.
4. *Big Book of AA*, p. 15, para. 2.
5. Ibid., p. 562–563.